THE H~~Y~~
DICTION~~ARY~~

At last – a perfect companion for both beginner hypochondriacs and more seasoned practitioners of the art. In easy-to-read, cross-referenced format, this essential volume lists words that will impress and symptoms that will fool your doctor every time. It gives the worst-case scenario that could arise from every tiny discomfort.

This book does what you've always wanted – it believes you. It takes your illnesses seriously.

SIMON BRETT is author of the bestselling *How to be a Little Sod*, the award-winning radio and television series, *After Henry*, and numerous extremely popular crime novels. His health at the time of going to press was fine.

DR SARAH BREWER writes the Dr Sarah column in the *Daily Mirror*. She is the author of *What Worries Women Most*, *The Body Awareness Programme* and co-author of *The Bluffer's Guide to Sex*. Sarah has been a hypochondriac from an early age and has trained all her patients accordingly.

Charts by Wendy Hutton, Swiderska Hutton Design

The Hypochondriac's Dictionary of Ill Health

Simon Brett
and
Dr Sarah Brewer

HEADLINE

Dedicated to everyone who has ever
worried about their health
(Go on, that includes you, doesn't it?)

Copyright © 1994 Simon Brett and Dr Sarah Brewer

The right of Simon Brett and Dr Sarah Brewer to be identified as the
Authors of the Work has been asserted by them in accordance
with the Copyright, Designs and Patents Act 1988.

First published in paperback in 1994
by HEADLINE BOOK PUBLISHING

10 9 8 7 6 5 4 3 2 1

All rights reserved. No part of this publication may be
reproduced, stored in a retrieval system, or transmitted,
in any form or by any means, without the prior written
permission of the publisher, nor be otherwise circulated
in any form of binding or cover other than that in which
it is published and without a similar condition being
imposed on the subsequent purchaser.

ISBN 0 7472 4699 8

Typeset by
Letterpart Limited, Reigate, Surrey

Printed and bound in Great Britain by
Cox & Wyman Ltd, Reading, Berks

HEADLINE BOOK PUBLISHING
A division of Hodder Headline PLC
338 Euston Road
London NW1 3BH

Introduction

At last – here is the book that the world of medicine has been waiting for since Hippocrates uttered his first oath. *The Hypochondriac's Dictionary of Ill Health* offers hope, support and factual back-up to everyone who has ever suffered the tiniest twinge of anxiety about their physical wellbeing.

In an easy-to-read, Hypochondriac-friendly alphabetical format, this invaluable book lists more Diseases than the most paranoid and fevered imagination could invent. It relates Symptoms to Illnesses, providing that outcome most desired by all Hypochondriacs: the Worst-Case Scenario. Now you need no longer worry that your ailments are trivial; in this book you will discover that even the most minor discomfort could be the harbinger of something Life-Threatening.

Illustrated with instructive diagrams and copiously cross-referenced, *The Hypochondriac's Dictionary of Ill Health* is the essential companion to medical panic. For ease of use, Symptoms which fool your GP every time have been helpfully marked with asterisks; Doctor-impressing words for common ailments are highlighted with the # symbol. Cross-references are in capitals.

Now you can put amateur health anxieties behind you. Armed with this book, you can confidently join the ranks of professional Hypochondria.

The Hypochondriac's Dictionary of Ill Health was compiled with you in mind. It guarantees you that comfort so often denied by uncaring members of the medical profession: this book really believes that you're genuinely ill.

So away you go. Start reading – and start worrying!

A

ABBREVIATIONS Medical notes were traditionally littered with these to protect Doctors who couldn't – or wouldn't – spell out what they meant. High Court judges now have the power to decipher abbreviations, and strangely, Doctors have stopped using gems such as:

TATSP	Thick As Two Short Planks
PBM	Poor Biological Material
TSSOAP	Three Sandwiches Short Of A Picnic
LOMBARD	Loads Of Money But A Right Dickhead
CAUC	Complete And Utter Clot
WOOS	Work Out Own Salvation (i.e., I am unable to help this patient).

ABDOMINAL PAIN* A good Hypochondriac's Symptom, because it's so easy to fake. Hold your tummy muscles rigid whilst the Doctor feels your abdomen (PALPATION). Groan a little and, with a bit of luck, he'll feel obliged to diagnose Peritonitis, a serious Inflammation of the abdominal cavity. It's worth knowing what is causing the abdominal pain you've chosen to present to your doctor – see diagram.

ABNORMALITY A physical deformity or unusual result. This is a strong medical word, which Doctors take seriously. The phrase 'Doctor, my bowels are abnormal' merits a complete work-up, entailing several visits to an enema unit. If a Doctor tells you your blood tests are abnormal, feel free to worry: he's probably right.

ABSCESS A collection of pus in any tissue of the body.

ABDOMINAL PAIN

The **hypochondriac's** guide to what certain kinds of abdominal pain could be symptomatic of...

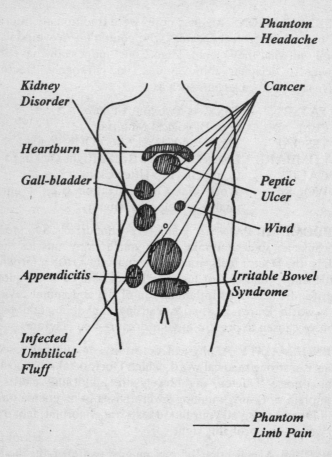

Phantom Headache

Kidney Disorder

Cancer

Heartburn

Gall-bladder

Peptic Ulcer

Wind

Appendicitis

Irritable Bowel Syndrome

Infected Umbilical Fluff

Phantom Limb Pain

Symptoms include Pain, Swelling, Fever, Surface Redness and often a feeling of intense pressure. Most Abscesses are treated by Surgical Drainage. A Surgeon holds his nose, punctures the site with a scalpel and then squeezes out the contents with relish. Many practise on relatives' blackheads.

ACCIDENTAL DEATH Accounts for a third of all deaths between the ages of five and thirty-four years. Some Doctors seem particularly prone to accidents – but are able to bury their mistakes.

ACNE Most Hypochondriacs can spot a spot before it's visible to anyone else. As a spot can, rarely, develop into something LIFE-THREATENING like a Collar-Stud Abscess, you might argue that even the most minuscule pimple needs treatment.

ACUPUNCTURE A type of Chinese medicine in which needles are inserted into precise points on the body to relieve Symptoms in totally different parts of the body. The principle is a bit like the Government's approach to the NHS – if they know there is suffering in one area, they immediately apply the remedy somewhere completely different.

ADDICTION An Addiction is a Dependence on a drug, accompanied by Cravings and unpleasant Symptoms (Cold Turkey) when the drug is withdrawn. The most addictive drugs known to man are: Opiates (e.g., Heroin), Cocaine, Crack, some sleeping tablets (e.g., Benzodiazepines), Alcohol, Nicotine and Caffeine. Addictions are good things to have, as you can often get compensation. Try becoming the first Hypochondriac to sue a coffee manufacturer.

ADENOIDS Mid-line glandular swellings at the back of the nose, above the tonsils. Adenoids usually shrink after the age of five and disappear by the time of puberty. 'Doctor, it's my Adenoids' – or, more likely, 'Doctor, it's my Adedoids' – will not go down well if you are a strapping great rugby player. But don't despair – it still might trigger a search for a Nasal Polyp.

ADIPOSE TISSUE Forty-five per cent of men and thirty-six per cent of women have too much adipose tissue – fat. The overweight Hypochondriac must insist their Doctor screens them for all sorts of hormonal problems. Mention that Hypothyroidism, Cushing's Syndrome, Prader-Willi Syndrome and Laurence-Moon-Biedl Syndrome all run in your family and you should quickly be referred to an Endocrinologist.

ADMINISTRATOR In the modern NHS, this is the person whose duty it is to run hospitals efficiently and see that beds are used only for the genuinely ill and not for those who just *might* be ill. As such, the Hypochondriac's natural enemy.

ADMISSION TO HOSPITAL An essential step on the road to Hypochondriac Nirvana.

ADRENALINE A Hormone secreted by the adrenal glands. High levels are triggered by Stress, Exercise and Fear. This speeds the heart, and often results in impromptu emptying of the bowels. If you suffer from chronic DIARRHOEA and excessive Flushing (both face and toilet cistern), ask if your Doctor has considered a diagnosis of Phaeochromocytoma (pronounced fee-o-kromo-site-oma – make sure you get it right, the Doctor'll be impressed) a type of adrenal gland Tumour.

AEROBICS A fitness regime characterised by the eruption of lividly coloured leotards. To be avoided by Hypochondriacs at all costs – it might do you some good.

AGORAPHOBIA Fear of open spaces. A Hypochondriac complaining of this has both advantages and disadvantages. It may help you achieve that ultimate concession from your Doctor – a HOUSE CALL. On the other hand, it means you miss all those hours in the WAITING ROOM picking up those useful new Symptoms that the other patients chatter on about.

AGUE Doctors may be old-fashioned, but don't go to yours complaining of this. Serve you right if he responds by prescribing that you hang three spiders in a leather bag around your neck. If you're really convinced you've got an Ague, cut down on your intake of Shakespeare.

ALBATROSS SYNDROME This refers to the patient hanging around the Surgeon's neck with numerous complaints following ill-chosen surgery. Derives from Coleridge's 'The Rime of the Ancient Mariner'. Remember the Hypochondriac's version of this poem, which begins:

It is a great new wonder drug,
And it stoppeth one of three,
But your other two bad side effects
Will still gain sympathy.

ALCOHOL WITHDRAWAL SYNDROME Should be a Doctor-impressing word for Hangover. Unfortunately, few Doctors are impressed by it.

ALEXIA WITHOUT AGRAPHIA SYNDROME Though it sounds like the title of a Greek tragedy, this is in fact a Neurological Disconnection Disorder where the right side of the brain doesn't know what the left is doing. A problem common among bureaucrats, British tennis players and the Conservative Party.

ALLERGY* An excellent catch-all explanation for more or less all Diseases. 'Maybe it's an Allergy, Doctor . . .?' is a question that should be frequently on the lips of Hypochondriacs. With a bit of luck, it will lead to exhaustive TESTS on virtually everything you eat, breathe, touch or go to bed with. The good news is that your Doctor will find it almost impossible to identify what you're *really* Allergic to – which is, of course, Getting Better.

AMBULANCE The ultimate status symbol. For a Hypochondriac, this is the equivalent of a stretch limo.

AMNESIA Not a good problem to have. For the Hypochondriac it raises the very real danger that you might forget your Symptoms before telling the Doctor about them – assuming you remembered to keep your appointment in the first place.

AMPUTATION The removal of a limb. Any Hypochondriac achieving this can be really sure that his or her complaint is being taken seriously.

ANAL FISSURE 1. A painful crack on the anal margin.
2. An angler of specified tastes.

ANAL FIXATION 1. See ANUS. (You'll probably need to use a mirror.)
2. An unfortunate side effect of sitting on spiked railings.

ANGINA PECTORIS A Symptom of Heart Disease, characterised by severe Pain behind the breast bone, sometimes spreading down the left arm, or even both arms. This is a good one for the Hypochondriac, because you don't have to reproduce the Symptoms in the surgery – just tell your

Doctor about the paroxysms of pain you felt in the relevant areas – be sure to mention that left arm – and you should be on for a few TESTS at the very least.

ANTERIOR CHEST WALL SYNDROME* This one is the Hypochondriac's dream. All you have to do is describe a sharp, localised tenderness felt in the muscles between the ribs at the front of the chest. Throw in the odd medical phrase such as 'Ow, I've got Precordial Catch', and you're home and dry. This Syndrome is often mistaken for ANGINA or even a Heart Attack, so should certainly be good for a few days off work.

ANTIBIOTICS Drugs originally derived from living organisms, whose effect is to curb the development of other organisms. These are the bottom line for Hypochondriacs. Under no circumstances do you leave your Doctor's surgery without at least a PRESCRIPTION for Antibiotics.

ANXIETY Permanent state of mind for the true Hypochondriac. If you should ever find yourself ceasing to be anxious, immediately open a Medical Dictionary and read through until you find a Symptom you haven't had before. Within seconds you should have developed it, and you will find that your Anxiety has miraculously returned.

APPENDICITIS Inflammation of, or sometimes Abscess on, the APPENDIX.

APPENDIX See back of book.

APPENDIX, GRUMBLING An ideal ailment for the Hypochondriac, because it can go on Grumbling just as long as you can. Beware, though, that your condition doesn't become APPENDICITIS, as this will lead to an Appendectomy, and then you'll have one less organ to Grumble about.

APPOINTMENT The first step on the ladder towards having your Symptoms taken seriously.

ARSENIC 1. Poison popular as murder method in Victorian times.
2. A cut in the posterior region (colloquial).

ARTIFICIAL INSEMINATION A method of inducing PREGNANCY which takes away all the fun.

ASPERGILLOSIS A Chest Infection caused when the lung is invaded by Fungi of the genus *Aspergillus*, which thrives on mouldy grain. Pigeon fanciers are particularly susceptible to this, because of their practice of passing grain from their mouths to young birds. People who indulge in practices like that – and who fancy pigeons – deserve everything that's coming to them.

ASPIRIN A synonym for Acetylsalicylic Acid, this is one of the most effective treatments for a wide variety of ailments. As such, it should be avoided by Hypochondriacs at all costs. Nothing sounds so dismisive from a Doctor as the order, 'Take two aspirins'. If your Doctor insists on recommending this, then at least ensure he says, 'Take two doses of Acetylsalicylic Acid', to preserve a little credibility.

AUTOSUGGESTION 1. A form of self-hypnotism, whereby an individual can really believe that he or she can feel imaginary Symptoms. As such, one of the Hypochondriac's favourite pastimes.
2. A proposition made by a boy to a girl in a car. Can lead to PREGNANCY.

B

BABINSKI'S SIGN This is a reliable indicator of the extent of Brain Damage present. Take a key (traditionally, that of a Bentley) and scratch the outer edge of your naked sole. If your big toe jumps upwards, the reflex is positive. Sell the Bentley to pay for a full Neurological Investigation.

BACK, BAD* Over 67 million working days are lost annually through Bad Backs in the UK alone, so it's a good complaint for a Hypochondriac to take to his or her doctor. All you have to do is point vaguely in the direction of your back and wince a lot. But do remember that when you walk out of the surgery clutching your sick note you must use the same crabwise, agonised gait you did when you came in.

BACTERIA Microscopic, single-celled organisms that cause problems out of all proportion to their size. Bacteria can be killed by ANTIBIOTICS unless they develop Resistance. Consult your Doctor about any twinge, throb, redness or slight Fever, in case you have a treatable Bacterial Infection. If it's not treatable, you go straight to the top of the Hypochondriac class – though probably not for long.

BALANITIS Literally, inflammation of the balan – which must be an obscure word meaning PENIS. This nasty little Infection – or large Infection, depending on your endowment – makes the end of the penis redder and more tender than usual. May be due to a Sexually Transmissible Disease, Allergy, Tight Foreskin, Thrush, or Excessive Reading of Tolkien.

BANDAGE 1. A long strip of clean material used to keep wound dressings in place, to stop bleeding or to support a Strain or Sprain.
2. A form of Sexual Deviation, similar to Bondage, in which the dominatrix is a Ward Sister (not difficult – they're all naturally that way).

BARRIER METHOD A form of Contraception which places a physical barrier between the sperm and the egg. This may take the form of a Condom, Diaphragm, Chastity Belt, Gear Lever or Chair Hitched Under The Doorknob.

'BEDSIDE MANNER' A solicitous and sympathetic concern from the medical profession that went out with Dr Finlay.

BENEFITS Payments made by the Government for a whole range of disabilities, illnesses and malingerings. Make sure you know which benefits you are entitled to – then immediately develop Symptoms of the Diseases that justify them.

BENIGN A Benign Growth is definitely non-Cancerous, though few Hypochondriacs ever believe this. If you are eventually persuaded that your Lump is Benign, take comfort from the fact that even Benign Growths can eventually turn MALIGNANT.

BETA BLOCKERS This class of drugs is used to treat everything from High Blood Pressure, Angina, Heart Attacks and Overactive Thyroids to Migraine, ANXIETY, Stage Fright and Driving Test Nerves. Hypochondriacs are advised to keep clear of them; if you start feeling all calm and relaxed, there's a very real danger of the worst possible disaster: you might stop worrying about your health.

BIOPSY A diagnostic TEST in which a fragment of tissue is removed and examined under the microscope to exclude

MALIGNANCY. Most Hypochondriacs would insist that a bit of every part of their body – including their dandruff – should be Biopsied just in case.

BIRTH See CHILDBIRTH (Any other kind was probably written by Stephen King). More babies are born in the sixth month after their parents' marriage than at any other time. Only five per cent of them enter the world at the time predicted by the medical profession (*cf.* BRITISH RAIL TIMETABLES).

BIRTHMARKS These vary in form, colour and shape. The level of embarrassment caused by them depends largely on location, and many of the most unsightly can be eradicated by cosmetic surgery. When someone tells you that a disfigurement on their features is a Birthmark, do not say, as President Reagan did to Mikhail Gorbachev, 'Oh, and how long have you had it?'

BLACK DEATH Between 1346 and 1351, this particularly virulent Disease (aka Bubonic Plague) destroyed about a third of the world's population. A visit to the surgery with symptoms of this is not recommended – even the stupidest Doctors may realise they're dealing with a Hypochondriac.

BLACKHEAD A black-capped plug of grease blocking the opening of a skin gland. These are particularly harrowing for Hypochondriacs – every one is a potential MALIGNANT MELANOMA. Your Doctor will understand if you book an appointment every Friday at 18.30pm to have your blackheads visually inspected against Malignant Change.

BLOOD A red substance that sends Hypochondriacs into paroxysms of hysteria. Any blood-stained Discharge should be reported to your Doctor immediately: it could mean your promotion from Hypochondriac to true sufferer of Disease.

BLOOD PRESSURE It is vitally important to know your Blood Pressure. A fit adult has a BP of around 120/80. At the sight of a specialist, it often goes higher – due to WHITE COAT HYPERTENSION. At the sight of a pretty Nurse or dishy Doc, it shoots right up (lust).

BODY ODOUR An unpleasant condition that only affects other people.

BORBORYGMI Embarrassing, audible bowel sounds caused by air and fluid rumbling through the bowels. Doctors use Borborygmi as a diagnostic tool. If sounds are high-pitched and tinkling, you may have Bowel Obstruction. If sounds are ominously absent, and accompanied by ABDOMINAL PAIN, you may have Peritonitis. If sounds are rhythmic and repetitive, going 'shick-a-boom shick-a-boom shick-a-boom', you may have swallowed a Walkman.

BOTTOM The use of this word in a Doctor's surgery is the mark of an amateur Hypochondriac, except in the one permissible sentence: 'I want to get to the bottom of this, Doctor.'

BOWELS Hypochondriacs have a duty to examine and record their daily bowel function. This is important, as a change in bowel habit is often the only sign that Colitis, IRRITABLE BOWEL SYNDROME or Colonic CANCER has developed. Use the Complete Stool Gazers Chart (see diagram) for a week, then take it to your Doctor for a full analysis.

BRACE 1. An orthodontic appliance to straighten wonky teeth.
2. An orthopaedic appliance to support part of the body, or hold it immobile.

BOWELS

STOOL GAZERS CHART

Day	1	2	3	4	5	6	7
Frequency							
Colour							
Consistency							
Texture							
Size							
Shape							
Odour							
Mucus							
Blood							
Sweetcorn							
Tomato Skins							

[Doctors on the whole prefer you to come to the surgery with a chart rather than with the actual examples.]

3. 'Brace yourself, Sheila!' – an Australian medical warning that an unpleasant, Invasive Examination is coming up.

BRAIN The most miraculous organ in a Hypochondriac's body, endlessly capable of inventing new Symptoms.

BREAST EXAMINATION Women should examine their breasts regularly for Lumps as they have a one in eleven chance of developing Breast Cancer. The examination is best done once a month after menstruation, though most Hypochondriacs prefer to do it every day – better still, every hour. One per cent of cases of Breast Cancer occur in men – so men should examine their breasts at the same time as they examine their TESTICLES.

BREATHING Not a good habit to stop.

BRUISING Frequently a very encouraging sign for Hypochondriacs, because it could mean you have all kinds of really serious illnesses. Take your pick from a Blood Clotting Disorder, Ageing Skin, Liver Disease, Drug Side Effects, Scurvy or even Leukaemia. Alternatively, Bruising could mean that your partner's finally had enough of you going on about your Symptoms all the time.

BYPASS SURGERY 1. Technique developed to bypass a Blockage by the replacement of part of a diseased artery with a bit from another part of the body – or with an artificial tube.
2. Technique developed by expert Hypochondriacs who manage to get referred straight to a Consultant without going through the boring bit of making an appointment with their GP.

C

CADAVER Most Hypochondriacs end up as one of these. A Cadaver is a human body used for medical research after death. You will find it gratifying to know that what was wrong with you during life frequently defies medical knowledge in the afterlife too.

CAFE AU LAIT SPOTS Although these might be due to spilling coffee on your skin, they can be a sign of Neurofibromatosis (Elephant Man's Disease). All Hypochondriacs should strip naked in front of a friend (or Doctor if all friends have deserted you) and have every coffee-coloured blemish counted. You are allowed up to five.

CANCER The Disease worshipped in hallowed tones by all true Hypochondriacs. You know it's going to get you. It's just a question of when.

CANDIDIASIS A popular Yeast Infestation, which homes in on parts of the body that are warm and moist (use your imagination). Your best defences against Candidiasis are Anti-Thrush diets, intimate rituals with Live Yoghurt, and hot-ironing pantie gussets.

CAPUT 1. The Latin word for head.
2. Medical word used to describe a Hypochondriac who might be quite poorly.

CARBUNCLE A collection of skin Boils, often on the neck, buttocks, groin or armpits. Usually not serious, but could be a sign of Diabetes or a faulty Immune System. Ask your

Doctor what your chances of having Lazy Leucocyte Syndrome are. If he doesn't seem impressed, ask about HIV instead.

CARCINOGEN An environmental agent capable of causing CANCER. Common Carcinogens are tobacco smoke, radiation, asbestos fibres, tar, Genital Wart Virus, soot and people in the Doctor's WAITING ROOM talking about Cancer.

CARDIAC ARREST See PRIVATE MEDICAL INSURANCE, COST OF.

CARDIAC NEUROSIS A psychological problem that affects Hypochondriacs lucky enough to have a real Heart Attack. Occasionally it afflicts those unlucky enough to have missed one. It is an obsessive ANXIETY concerning the state of the heart. If you're a Hypochondriac suffering from this, you must stick to your guns, otherwise kindly medics will try to rehabilitate you into a normal, active lifestyle.

CASTRATION Surgical removal of the TESTICLES. If you only went in for a VASECTOMY, look for dollar signs floating in front of your eyes. See MEDICO-LEGAL COMPENSATION.

CATHARSIS A form of purification. Cathartic drugs purify the bowel – by forcing all its contents into the sewers in five seconds flat. Freud used Psychological Catharsis, under the power of Hypnosis or Psychodrama, to relive forgotten memories and unpleasant experiences – such as emptying your bowels into the sewer in five seconds flat.

CATHETERISATION Best avoided if at all possible. It involves stuffing a wide tube into the bladder through the URETHRA. In women, this only involves 2-3cm of tubing. In the male, 15-20cm (some men boast 30cm) is traversed.

Induces a sensation that makes the legs, eyes, fingers and bowels cross all at the same time.

CELLS, LITTLE GREY Brain cells, liable, in Hercule Poirot, to cause sudden, intuitive leaps of brilliant logic; and, in John Major, to produce little grey ideas.

CEREBELLAR ATAXIA A jerky, staggering way of walking due to Brain Damage. An ideal defence if anyone accuses you of being drunk. All you have to do is say, 'No, officer, I suffer from Hereditary Cerebellar Ataxia.' Unfortunately that is not as easy as it sounds.

CERVICAL SMEAR The gentle removal of loose surface cells from the CERVIX to check for early, pre-Cancerous changes. This Investigation is so useful, female Hypochondriacs should try to have it at least once per year. Your Doctor won't mind – he gets paid vast amounts of money for even pretending he's done one.

CERVIX The lower segment of the uterus (womb), which becomes dilated during CHILDBIRTH. After Childbirth it soon returns to approximately its original size. (Normal cervix will be resumed as soon as possible.)

CHAGA'S DISEASE A Sleeping Sickness caused by a Trypanosome Parasite, spread by insects called Assassin Bugs. Not a good disease for a Hypochondriac to claim to have; since it is pronounced Shagger's Disease, misunderstandings are inevitable.

CHEST PAIN* Usually good for at least a few days off sick. A tight Chest Pain, like a bear hug, which radiates down your left arm and up into your left jaw warrants a few days' in the Intensive Care unit. Even if your Blood Tests and Heart Tracing are normal, firmly remind your Doctor that this cannot exclude a MYOCARDIAL INFARCTION. You should get a good six weeks off work. See ANGINA PECTORIS; CARDIAC NEUROSIS.

CHILDBIRTH Usually easy to spot when imminent. Good for several months' maternity leave – and occasionally paternity leave as well. Other BENEFITS are quite good too, though you do tend to end up holding the baby.

CHILDBIRTH, NATURAL Involves a lot of puffing and panting and little in the way of drugs or monitors. Relaxation Techniques are the mainstay of controlling Pain, until it really gets going, when many expectant mothers tell their husbands to stop singing bloody nursery rhymes and find the bloody Doctor to organise an EPIDURAL.

CHILL Something all Hypochondriacs catch, despite little medical evidence that such an ailment exists. A Chill often precedes a FEVER. All Chills, Fevers and someone walking over your grave should be investigated immediately. In the latter case, consider the possibility that you might be a CADAVER.

CHOLECYSTECTOMY Surgical removal of the gall-bladder. As gall-bladder problems cause pain under the right ribs, the classic site of all Hypochondriac Pain, you can often spot a true Hypochondriac by the little zipper (scar) in their upper right abdominal quadrant. It's worth comparing surgical stitching techniques at jacuzzi parties.

CHORDEE Abnormal curvature of the PENIS, usually downwards. See BANANAS ARE NOT THE ONLY FRUIT.

CHRONIC* The Hypochondriac's favourite word. To a true sufferer, 'something chronic' means unbearable Pain. Unfortunately, this is where Doctor-patient communication breaks down. A Doctor thinks of CHRONIC as meaning the Latin derivation – having lasted a long time.

CIRCUMCISION The unkindest cut of all. Circumcision is a good thing for male Hypochondriacs as it reduces the risk of Penile Cancer (though of course at the same time it's a bad thing, as it gives you one less Disease to worry about). Circumcised males with second thoughts may now get a second foreskin. A stretching technique perfected in the United States pulls the remaining endowment downwards with a specially shaped adhesive plaster. It takes up to six years for a complete foreskin to regrow – and then you'll be ready to get circumcised again!

CIRRHOSIS Don't say you've got this as it implies Alcohol Abuse. The alternative is to tell people you suffer from Chronic Hepatitis, Biliary Cirrhosis, Haemochromatosis or Wilson's Disease – none of which are easy to do when you're drunk.

CLERGYMAN'S KNEE Male version of Housemaid's Knee (demonstrating how undervalued the clergy are in the social pecking order – and raising the interesting question of what women priests will call this ailment when they get it).

COFFIN That dream retirement home all Hypochondriacs aspire to.

COITUS INTERRUPTUS Frustrated sexual intercourse. (See CONTRACEPTION; CHILDREN COMING INTO PARENTAL BED; UNEXPECTED EARLY RETURN OF SPOUSE FROM BUSINESS TRIP.)

COMA A state of deep Unconsciousness or Stupor – not a common affliction for the Hypochondriac to suffer. After all, what's the use of an illness which renders you incapable of

19

complaining about your Symptoms?

COMEDO# Doctor-impressing word for a BLACKHEAD.

COMMON COLD No Hypochondriac ever suffers from a Common Cold. It should always be a point of honour for you to come up with a better name for what you've got. Have a go at Coryza, or a rare, LIFE-THREATENING, necrotising INFLUENZA.

COMMUNITY VIRUS No self-respecting Hypochondriac will allow him or herself to be fobbed off with this as a Diagnosis. All the Doctor is saying is 'I haven't a clue what's wrong with you, but there's a lot of it about.' See TALOIA.

COMPLICATIONS All Hypochondriacs' illnesses, by definition, have Complications.

CONFIDENTIALITY Something a Hypochondriac demands of his or her Physician – except on those occasions when you've come up with a really original illness which has medical science baffled. Any Hypochondriac would be flattered by the image of a Doctor saying to his expert colleagues at the Royal Society of Medicine, 'You know, a patient came to me today with something that's *really* got me stumped. Don't know if any of you have any ideas on what it might be . . .?'

CONSENT Something you must sign before the first of your Surgical Investigations and trials of treatment. Make sure you read the small print. Phrases such as 'This treatment will make you go blind, grow hairs on your palm and turn you stark raving mad' may require further inquiry.

CONSTIPATION See BOWELS. The World Constipation

Record is 102 days. No Hypochondriac should bother trying to beat this.

CONSULTANT Doctor who is more expensively ignorant of what's wrong with you than your GP.

CONTAGIOUS Assume that everyone you meet is Contagious unless you have irrefutable proof to the contrary.

CONVALESCENCE The Hypochondriac's holiday. Convalescence is an idyllic period of rest and recuperation, during which you still have the official sanction of Having Been Ill with plenty of time to make up your mind about What You're Going To Be Ill With Next.

CORONARY THROMBOSIS When this occurs, the arteries supplying the heart muscles become blocked, and insufficient blood passes through them. As the largest single killer of men in the Western world, Coronary Thrombosis is clearly something of which the dedicated Hypochondriac should be aware. But try not to have one until you're certain you really have exhausted all other Symptoms in your Medical Dictionary.

CORYZA# Doctor-impressing medical name for the COMMON COLD. A good word for Hypochondriacs to flaunt among their friends; less useful in conversations with Doctors, who tend to know that's all it means.

CRISIS It is a point of honour for the true Hypochondriac always to make a drama out of a Crisis. In medical terms, the Crisis marked the turning point in an Infective Disease before the advent of Antibiotics. By definition, Hypochondriacal Crises always turn out for the worse.

CRUTCH PALSY Temporary weakness or paralysis of the

wrist, fingers and thumb due to pressure in the armpit from using a too-tall crutch. It can also develop if you fall asleep with your arm over the back of a chair. In spite of its name, this will have no adverse effect on your sex life.

CURE Something to be avoided by Hypochondriacs at all times. When a Cure for any complaint becomes inevitable, the true Hypochondriac will within seconds have come up with a whole new set of Symptoms for something entirely different.

CURE-ALL An even more appalling concept for Hypochondriacs.

D

DTs Delirium Tremens. Profound Tremor, Confusion and Hallucinations caused by withdrawal of Alcohol.

DDTs Dreadful Delirium Tremens. Profound Tremor, Confusion and Hallucinations caused by withdrawal of Insecticide.

DAY HOSPITAL Anathema to all Hypochondriacs. Any Disease worth its salt merits at least an overnight stay in Intensive Care. The one saving grace of the Day Hospital is that it is a more satisfying place to have TESTS than the local GP's surgery.

DEATH The ultimate terminus of any Disease. Diagnosed when all the body's Vital Functions have ceased. Death is surprisingly difficult to diagnose, especially amongst politicians. Hypochondriacs should, in the first instance, request a COFFIN with an integral alarm system rather than cremation. A safer option is to become a CADAVER. That way, if you do wake up unexpectedly, you'll be in a teaching hospital full of highly qualified Doctors eager to write you up in the *British Medical Journal*.

DEATH CERTIFICATE The Hypochondriac's ultimate justification.

DEATH'S DOOR, AT A colourful expression to describe a truly LIFE-THREATENING condition. If an anxious wife is told that her husband is 'at Death's Door', a sensitive nurse will then add, 'But I'm sure the Doctor can pull him through'.

23

DECOMPENSATION 1. Extreme Heart Failure when the muscle gives up even trying to cope.
2. Removal of health insurance from a Hypochondriac due to excessive and repeated claims.

DECUBITUS A medical word meaning 'lying down'. Hypochondriacs are advised to be cautious in the use of the phrase. Their image as people with a wide knowledge of medicine will be enhanced, for example, if they refer to a Bed Sore as a Decubitus Ulcer. But they'll be shown up if they start saying things like 'I'm not feeling well – I think I should be decubitus', or 'I won't take this decubitus'.

DEFIBRILLATION Desperate, last-ditch attempt to revive a dead heart using Electric Shock Treatment. Most famous (and rich) Hypochondriacs keep a Defibrillator (See MACHINE WHICH GOES PING!) at home for unexpected emergencies.

DEHISCENCE# Doctor-impressing word meaning splitting open of a partly healed wound. If Abdominal Scars dehisce, there is a danger of the guts falling out or Infection getting in. Even a small cut on the finger can dehisce – so get every wound checked by your doctor in case it needs stitching, taping, supergluing or bandaging.

DEJA VU A French phrase meaning 'already seen' – an intense feeling of familiarity as if one had experienced the identical event before. Déja vu is regularly experienced by Doctors when Hypochondriacs enter their surgeries.

DELIRIUM A Brain Disturbance, characterised by incoherent speech and uncontrolled muscular actions. See PATRICK MOORE, DAVID BELLAMY.

DEMENTIA An Organic Brain Syndrome characterised by

a general decline in all areas of mental function. If, as you read this, you think you're suffering from dementia, don't worry. You will have forgotten all about it by the time you've moved on to the next entry.

DENDRITES Small tendrils branching out from nerve cells to allow communication with surrounding NEURONS. If your Doctor mutters that you only possess two Dentrites and one SYNAPSE – a polite medical way of saying you're TATSP, Thick As Two Short Planks – tell him you won't take it DECUBITUS.

DEPRESSION Feelings of sadness (the Blues) usually accompanied by EARLY MORNING WAKING, loss of libido, poor appetite and weight loss. Usually occurs out of the blue for no reason. GPs are now much more understanding about Depression than they used to be – which is hardly surprising, given the way the NHS is going.

DERMATITIS Nasty Inflammation of the skin. As this could be due to an Allergy to chemicals used at work (e.g., detergent, ink, morning coffee) it's best to get a long-term sick note to let Dermatitis settle down. In the meantime, call the environmental health people to get even with your boss.

DERMOTITIS Nasty Inflammation of the skin (in Ireland).

DESIGNER DRUGS 1. Illegal chemicals designed to mimic the effects of other controlled drugs.
2. Psychedelic prescriptions provided by a Doctor in a natty suit.

DEVIATION, SEXUAL Obsolete term. Nowadays anything inside, outside, above, below, upside down or hanging from the chandeliers is considered within the norm of sexual behaviour – even if it involves a gerbil, superglue, shoe laces and a vacuum cleaner.

DEXTROCARDIA The Hypochondriac's ultimate practical joke. This is a rare condition in which the heart is situated in the right side of the chest instead of the left. Fools Doctors every time. Generally you can persuade them to cancel the DEATH CERTIFICATE and reverse the election to become a CADAVER.

DIABETES MELLITUS A common Disease in which sugar builds up in the blood due to insufficient INSULIN production in the pancreas. Symptoms include Tiredness (See TATT), POLYDIPSIA, Polyuria (passing excessive amounts of urine), blurred vision, hunger and weight loss. The existence of Diabetes is proved by checking the urine for sugar. Your chance of developing the Disease is one in a thousand, so always produce a fresh sample of urine whenever you visit the surgery.

NB: Doctors prefer you to bring it with you in a container, rather than improvising in the WAITING ROOM.

DIAGNOSIS A unique blend of art, science, experience, creativity and intuition which Doctors possess to a greater or lesser degree. Hypochondriacs reach a Diagnosis more quickly, via a straighter and more creative route than any qualified Physician, and with the help of no equipment more sophisticated than a Medical Dictionary. As the NHS has now adopted the rules of the market place, it's worth insisting that 'the customer is always right' when your own DIY Diagnosis is pooh-poohed.

DIARRHOEA The only thing worse than suffering from this is having to spell it. In Diarrhoea, bowel movements increase in fluidity, frequency and volume. If you feel as though the world is falling out of your BOTTOM, you're probably right. Diarrhoea may be a sign of a serious intestinal disorder, such as Ulcerative Colitis, Crohn's Disease, Obstruction With Overflow or CANCER, especially if it is CHRONIC or mixed with BLOOD and/or mucus. Always let your Doctor know if your BOWELS are loose, and offer to deliver a hot stool sample for culture.

DIET Self-imposed nutritional misery aimed at losing excess weight. As dieting is a full-time occupation, leaving little room for contemplation of Health, most Hypochondriacs avoid it like the plague. They do, however, recognise the place of faddish diets to counteract their ALLERGIES.

DIETETICS The use of nutritional science to maintain or restore health. As Dietetics involves a detailed knowledge of the composition of food and the psychological aspects of eating, most Hypochondriacs are great experts on the subject. After all, what Hypochondriac doesn't know which food stirs up their Indigestion, which causes Wind, and which is liable to set off their liver?

DIGESTION The processing of dietary nutrients to maintain and fuel the body. Starts in the mouth and ends in the toilet pan. Digestive disorders are the commonest problems suffered by Hypochondriacs. See BOWELS; HYPOCHONDRIUM; INDIGESTION; IRRITABLE BOWEL SYNDROME; LEFT ILIAC FOSSA.

DILATOR Frighteningly impassive, cold, stainless-steel instrument used to dilate a narrowed body cavity, tube or opening. Makes your eyes water just to look at the thing. See CATHETERISATION; URETHRA.

DISABILITY Politically incorrect word for what is now called 'different ability'.

DISABLED What you will become if you call a disabled person 'differently abled' to his face.

DISEASE If you're saddled with a Disease, bad luck. Your Symptoms date from the nineteenth century or before. Try changing them. SYNDROMES date from the twentieth century and are much classier.

DISC, INTERVERTEBRAL, PROLAPSED* (Also known as SLIPPED DISC.) The scourge of the medical profession and Hypochondriacs alike. The only people to like Slipped Intervertebral Discs are Chiropractors and Osteopaths, who make a career out of massaging, nudging, manipulating or forcing them back into place. Good for several weeks off work. If you suffer from a Prolapsed, Intervertebral Disc, never:

A)   Abbreviate this to PID if you are female (see PID)
B)   Say you have a PROLAPSE – unless you want all eyes to swivel instantly to your groin region.

DISLOCATION 1. Complete displacement of the two bones compiling a joint. Liable to attract minimum sympathy if contracted on-piste, off-piste, or when pissed.
2. Inability to remember whose bed you've woken up in after an unmemorable night on the tiles.

DISPLACEMENT ACTIVITY Transference of feelings from one object or person to another – e.g., hitting a wall when angry with the wife; falling in love with the Psychoanalyst who's repairing the damage left by your last affair. Hypochondriacs frequently vent their hatred, love or spleen on at least one of their many Doctors. Try not to choose a

Proctologist (bum specialist). You never know exactly where he's been – but you can always make a good guess at where he wants to go next.

DIVERTICULITIS Inflammation of bowel Diverticulae. This should always be taken seriously and treated with Antibiotics. If your Doctor is loath to advise more than Paracetamol for your abdominal twinge, burst forth on the dangers of Diverticulitis developing into a PERFORATION, ABSCESS, Peritonitis or even a Fistula.

DOCTOR A white-coated professional able to shuffle differential Diagnoses and autograph DEATH CERTIFICATES. As a famous Hypochondriac once said, 'It's not who your Doctor is but who you vote for that most affects your health.'

DOUBLE-BLIND 1. A type of controlled trial in which your Doctor may try to enrol you as a GUINEA PIG. Might also be one of the carefully concealed SIDE EFFECTS of said trial. Always read the small print carefully.
2. See MASTURBATION, EXCESSIVE.

DRIP Intravenous administration of fluid via equipment that is guaranteed to draw sympathy from a Hypochondriac's hardest-hearted relative.

DROPSY A favourite Disease of Hypochondriacs over the last few centuries. Now wildly out of date. Update your problem to Oedema.

DRUGS Powerful chemical substances that have specific, usually desirable, actions in the body. As a Hypochondriac, you either love 'em or you hate 'em. On the one hand, they give credit to the validity of your illness; on the other, they may CURE it. Comfort yourself with the thought of all those nasty SIDE EFFECTS.

DUMPING SYNDROME 1. Symptoms caused by the rapid passage of food into the upper intestine after an operation to remove part of the stomach.
2. Tendency of Doctors to offload their Hypochondriac patients on to as many Consultants as it takes to get you out of their hair.

DUPYTREN'S CONTRACTURE Though this sounds as if it ought to be the title of a film by Peter Greenaway, it is in fact the gradual bending-down of one or more fingers into the palm due to Fibrosis, which tethers the finger tendons. The cause is unknown, but it is more common in people with CIRRHOSIS. If your job entails manual labour, keep pestering your Surgeon until he promises to give you a Z-Plasty (a Z-shaped cut to relieve a Contracture of the hand).

DYSENTRY A nasty case of DIARRHOEA. The liquid stools are an impressionist's dream, colourfully mixed with blood, pus, and slime.

DYSLEXIA A reading and writing disability in which written symbols are otfen tranpsosed.

DYSPNOEA# Doctor-impressing word for Shortness of Breath.

E

ECG Electrocardiogram or Heart Tracing. If you're booked in for an ECG, make sure you don't get ECT instead. See MACHINE THAT GOES PING! and diagram.

ECT Electroconvulsive Therapy. The equivalent of shuffle and redeal using brain cells instead of playing cards.

EEG Electroencephalogram or Brain Wave Tracing. This TEST falls down with Hypochondriacs, as some Brain Activity is needed before the MACHINE GOES PING.

EAR, CAULIFLOWER Painful, swollen, disfiguration of the ear. This is followed by degeneration of cartilage, so the ear supposedly looks like a cauliflower. They obviously have strange cauliflowers in some parts of the country.

EAR, FOREIGN BODY IN Persuade the Spanish lodger to get his tongue out.

EARLY MORNING WAKING Common Symptom of DEPRESSION. Sufferers tend to wake at 02.00 – 03.00am or at 04.00 – 06.00am. Difficult to diagnose in shift workers, milkmen and rock stars.

ECHOLALIA The compulsive repetition of what another person has just said, just said, just said, just said.

ECTASIA 1. An impressive medical word meaning Dilation, usually of a duct carrying SECRETIONS from a GLAND.
2. Drug bought by dyslexic.

-ECTOMY Medical suffix meaning 'removal of'. As in:

ELECTROCARDIOGRAM

Interpretation of monitor signals

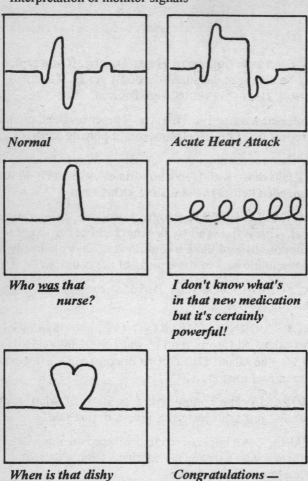

Normal

Acute Heart Attack

Who <u>was</u> that nurse?

I don't know what's in that new medication but it's certainly powerful!

When is that dishy doctor going to notice me?

Congratulations — you <u>were</u> ill.

Hysterectomy – removal of the hyster (womb)
Oophorectomy – removal of the oophor (ovary)
Lumpectomy – removal of a Lump
Hypochondrectomy – removal (with enormous relief)
    of a HEARTSINK PATIENT from a Doctor's list.

ECTOPIC A medical word that describes something occurring in an abnormal location or an activity occurring at an abnormal time, e.g.:

A) Ectopic Heartbeat – an extra, thumping contraction of the heart out of sequence with the preceding pulse rhythm.

B) Ectopic Pregnancy – implantation of a fertilised egg somewhere other than the womb.

C) Ectopic Medical Student – one found in bed with Nurse in Nurses' Home at 3.00am.

ECZEMA The same thing as DERMATITIS, but sounding more impressive. Don't go for the usual, boring Atopic (Allergic) Eczema. Try claiming Nummular or Discoid Eczema instead. As the cause of these red, scaly, disc-shaped skin LESIONS is unknown, try mentioning SELENIUM DEFICIENCY too. Bear your industrial disease compensation in mind, and shift back to Atopic Eczema when necessary.

ECDYSIS Veterinary word meaning sloughing of skin – usually as one whole piece. Rare in humans, but could be mistaken for chronic dandruff.

EJACULATION 1. Unexpected emission of sound from the mouth.
2. Expected emission of semen from the PENIS. See PREMATURE EJACULATION – but you'll have to be quick.

ELECTRIC SHOCK TREATMENT See DEFIBRILLATION;

ECT; MOST RECENT ELECTRICITY BILL INCLUSIVE OF VAT.

EMBOLUS A Wandering Clot (See HOSPITAL VISITOR). This is a serious condition in which an Internal Blood Clot or other particle travels in the circulation. When it impacts, it suddenly blocks the blood flow. The commonest Emboli affect the lungs, causing Shortness of Breath or impact in the brain leading to a Stroke or a Temporary Ischaemic Attack (see TIA). If you suspect you have an Embolism, admit yourself to Intensive Care without delay. If necessary, impersonate a visiting ADMINISTRATOR to ensure a bed is available.

EMBROCATION Veterinary ointment used on horses. Doctors sometimes fob these off on to unsuspecting Hypochondriacs too. It's time to wise up. Refuse the Embrocation and insist on a Topical Non-Steroidal Anti-inflammatory With Oral Back-up.

EMERGENCY Any crisis in which you feel medical intervention appropriate. It's not your fault if your definition of Emergency doesn't fit that of the GP's. After all, he's had a bit more training than you. Carry on calling him out in all weathers at any time of day or night. It's your Health and credibility that's at stake – not his.

EMESIS# Doctor-impressing word for Vomiting.

EMOLLIENT 1. Soothing, softening balm applied to the skin, eyes or mucous membranes.
2. Unctuous, patronising tone of a Consultant explaining that he can find nothing organically wrong with you. This is clearly his problem, not yours – he's just not looking hard enough.

ENCEPHALITIS Inflammation of the brain, usually due to

a VIRUS. Causes HEADACHE, FEVER, VOMITING and Drowsiness, which can progress to Confusion, Paralysis, Fits and COMA. If you notice any of these Symptoms, seek help straight away just in case.

Tip: Refuse the brain BIOPSY.

ENCOPRESIS A fascination with faeces, such that they are voided in socially unacceptable places – commonly the vicar's wellies. Guarantees at least three consultations with a PSYCHIATRIST. Encoprese into *his* wellies and you'll qualify for a second opinion.

ENDOCRINE SYSTEM* The collection of Hormone-secreting GLANDS that maintains normal body functioning. Endocrine Imbalances lead to a wide number of both common and obscure Diseases. You're always on safe ground claiming that your Symptoms result from Endocrine Malfunction – it could mean anything.

ENDOGENOUS Meaning 'arising from within the body'. Claim an Endogenous problem and you'll get loads of sympathy every time.

ENEMA Depending on the type of fluid poured into the back passage, Enemas may outline bowel walls prior to X-ray, deliver medication or empty the bowel of all its contents.

ENEMA, UNNECESSARY One of the few forms of revenge on Hypochondriacs available to the medical and nursing professions. To know when you're being given an Unnecessary Enema, watch out for the tell-tale bottle of Jeyes Fluid, tin of Golden Syrup, aerosol of Crazy Foam or single daffodil.

ENGORGEMENT Impressive word meaning stuffed right to

the brim. In medical terms, the organs most commonly engorged are lactating breasts and the PENIS – though rarely for the same reason.

ENTERIC-COATED The type of tablet all Hypochondriacs should insist on. Otherwise there is a danger of uncoated MEDICATION burning a hole in your stomach lining. See ULCER.

EPIDEMIOLOGY The numerical science which is obsessed with counting the Incidence, Prevalence and Causes of Disease. Without Hypochondriacs to swell the diagnostic numbers, Epidemiologists would be out of a job.

EPIDIDYMIS The long, coiled, squidgy tube attached to the top of the testicle at the back. As this is a favourite site for Cysts to develop, all male Hypochondriacs should examine their Epididymis and TESTICLES regularly.
Tip: Best not to do this in Sainsbury's.

EPIDURAL An excellent method of Spinal Analgesia for Hypochondriacs, popular during CHILDBIRTH. An Epidural takes away Pain and most sensations from the waist down. Whilst removing discomfort during an operation, it provides plenty of scope for post-Epidural tingling, numbness, headache and lightning pains long after the event. See MEDICO-LEGAL COMPENSATION.

EPISIOTOMY A surgical incision made in the paper-thin, stretched entrance to the vagina whilst a woman is giving birth to a large baby. Although it makes delivery easier, an Episiotomy demands a surgeon skilled in crochet and jig-saw puzzles to cobble it back together. Good for on-going Perineal Discomfort if you need an excuse other than a HEADACHE to avoid sex.

EPISTAXIS# Doctor-impressing word for a Nose Bleed.

EPITAPH The most famous Hypochondriac's Epitaph – and the one that all Hypochondriacs should endeavour to have engraved on their tombstones – is:
'SEE – I TOLD YOU I WAS ILL.'

ERECTION Method by which man reproduces his own kind. Inflation of the PENIS occurs by the same principle that keeps the lowly earthworm long, thin and wiggly – the hydrostatic skeleton.
NB: Experts in the art of seduction advise that mentioning this analogy at the moment of Erection tends to dampen the ardour of the female participant.

ERYSIPELAS A spreading Infection, usually of the face, similar to Cellulitis. Fever, Headache and itchy, red LESIONS occur. Tiny pimples and Blisters give the face the texture of bloody orange peel. Antibiotics are vital.
Tip: Don't wear red – you'll clash horribly and confuse the doctor.

ERYTHEMA INFECTIOSUM A childhood viral illness also known as Fifth Disease, or Slapped Cheek Syndrome. Red slap-like LESIONS occur on the face and can spread to the limbs. If your child develops this, call the Doctor quick and keep well out of the sight of social workers.

ESCHAR# Doctor-impressing word for Scab (not recommended for use in Trades Union disputes).

ETHICS, MEDICAL The professional code which insists that a doctor continues to examine, investigate, refer and even talk to a fully paid-up Hypochondriac.

EUTHANASIA The act of killing a person painlessly to

37

relieve suffering. Luckily for Hypochondriacs, this is illegal in most countries to prevent pruning of the HEARTSINK PATIENT population.

EXCORIATION# Doctor-impressing word for a Scratch.

EXCRETION Any unpleasant waste material voided by the body – ideally in private. See BOWELS.

EXPECTORANT 1. A cough remedy that encourages the coughing up of phlegm.
2. Misnomer for a pregnant woman.

EYE, FOREIGN BODY IN Ask the Spanish lodger to leave your lids alone now he's vacated your ear. See EAR, FOREIGN BODY IN.

F

FAINTING Temporary Loss of Consciousness due to lack of oxygen to the brain. Often attributed to Hysteria and Shock, but can indicate serious illness such as Dehydration, Anaemia, Irregular Heart Beat, Low Blood Pressure or abnormal Blood Sugar Levels. If you collapse, don't be fobbed off with just a Faint. If no one witnessed it, how can they be so sure you don't have Epilepsy?

FAITH HEALING The ability of some practitioners to cure Disease using a healing force that is inexplicable to science. The opposite of Faith Diseasing – the ability of Hypochondriacs to convince themselves they're ill when no ORGANIC cause is found. See FUNCTIONAL DISORDER.

FALLOPIAN TUBE Dark, winding Lovers' Lane for the sperm and egg. See PID and diagram.

FAMILIAL MEDITERRANEAN FEVER* An inherited condition amongst Mediterranean races with no known cause, diagnostic factor or specific treatment. Symptoms include recurrent FEVER, Arthritis, ABDOMINAL and CHEST PAIN. Sometimes red skin swellings or psychiatric Symptoms develop too. If you want an unusual disease that your Physician hasn't heard of – and can't prove you don't have – this could be a nice little rest-earner.

FARMER'S LUNG An occupational, respiratory Disease triggered by an Allergy to moulds on hay, straw or grains. Anyone who's ever visited a farm and subsequently developed a sniffle might be a candidate. At the very least, you

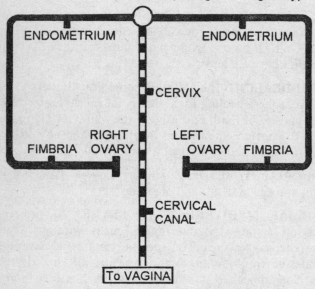

FALLOPIAN
TUBE MAP

UTERUS (Change for Pregnancy)

ENDOMETRIUM   ENDOMETRIUM

CERVIX

RIGHT   LEFT
FIMBRIA   OVARY   OVARY   FIMBRIA

CERVICAL
CANAL

To VAGINA

FEMALE

need a chest X-ray and Blood Tests to look for Specific Fungal Antibodies.

FATIGUE The more Hypochondriac-friendly term for Tiredness. Never admit to Tiredness – always insist on Extreme Fatigue – or, even better, MYALGIC ENCEPHALO-MYELITIS. See TATT.

FEBRILE Racked with FEVER. In some cases, overheating leads to Febrile Fits, especially in young children. Any hint of a Temperature requires urgent medical advice. Platitude to quote over the phone to a Doctor in a mysterious tone: 'You can never be too careful with a fever . . .'

FEMUR, FRACTURE OF Common Injury to the hip, especially in elderly ladies with Osteoporosis. One in four women will have suffered this fracture by the age of ninety, so if Granny falls over, always call out the doctor. After he's thoroughly examined you, let him have a cursory glance at Granny.

FETISHISM The use of special objects to achieve sexual arousal. Common practices involve rubber gloves, clogs, leather garments, plastic bags and parts of the body such as feet and ears. See EYE, FOREIGN BODY IN; SUPERGLUE SOLVENT.

FEVER Far too ordinary a word to be used by a Hypochondriac. If you've got a Fever, tell your Doctor it's Pyrexia.

FIBROADENOMA A BENIGN, fibrous Tumour found in the breast – affectionately known as a Breast Mouse. Hypochondriacs will not accept a diagnosis of Fibroadenoma without the bare minimum of a Mammography, a BIOPSY and a stiff gin.

FIBROSITIS A bit of a cop-out so far as Diagnosis is concerned. This is a non-medical term that describes non-specific Muscular Pain and stiffness. If your Doctor suggests you have Fibrositis, then he clearly lacks imagination. Refuse to leave the surgery until he comes up with something better.

FIRST AID For a Hypochondriac, this is undoubtedly a Medical Dictionary. When you run out of inspiration, you can always find another Disease in there for which you can quickly develop the Symptoms.

FITNESS An intangible quality that denotes a capacity for physical work and the performance of normal, daily activities without exhaustion. Most Hypochondriacs are physically, if not mentally, fit. The best way to ensure fitness is to choose the right parents and inherit fit and healthy genes – that's a big help, isn't it?

FLAT LINE The effect on a MACHINE THAT GOES PING! to which the Hypochondriac in INTENSIVE CARE aspires, at the same time hoping never quite to reach. While a Flat Line on the monitor will make the point that you really were ill, it will deprive you of the future pleasure of unearthing yet more exciting Symptoms. If, on the other hand, you get down to a line that's nearly flat and then start blipping again, this will give you the opportunity later to bore everyone to tears with your 'OUT-OF-BODY EXPERIENCE'.

FLATULENCE Abdominal Distension relieved by breaking wind. If you're lucky, this is upwards in private. If unlucky, this is downwards in public and accompanied by a roll of drums and the smell of rotting cabbage. In such circumstances, Hypochondriacs behave just as everyone else does –

i.e., they look with pained reproach at the person next to them. See BORBORYGMI.

FLATUS Medical term designed to take the wind out of the sails of a Fart. Excessive Flatus might be a sign of INDIGESTION, IRRITABLE BOWEL SYNDROME, GALL-BLADDER Disease or eating too many beans. If you can trap Flatus in a glass bottle this might aid your Doctor in formulating a Diagnosis.

FLUCTUANT A lovely word that describes movement felt within a Swelling when prodded. This indicates that the Swelling contains liquid such as pus – e.g., in an ABSCESS. If you want to know what Fluctuation feels like, try Palpating a water bed.

FLUKE 1. A parasitic flatworm.
2. The likely cause of your Doctor finding a plausible Diagnosis that even vaguely fits your Symptoms.

FOLLICULITIS Inflammation of hair follicles. Commonly occurs in the armpit, groin, buttocks, neck and beard. May develop into unsightly Pustules. Antibiotics are needed – plus scrupulous hygiene to prevent a major outbreak. You'll know if your pimple is likely to be infectious – the Doctor will back away from you in an attempt to avoid physical contact. When this happens, it's time to start worrying – though of course, being a Hypochondriac, you were anyway.

FOOD ADDITIVES* These sitting ducks may be safely blamed for any Symptom you care to mention. Try following an Additive-free Diet if you wish, but you do realise that involves no beefburgers, no Coke, no baked beans, no chocolate and no lager?

FOOD ALLERGY* A state-of-the-art cause for most

obscure Symptoms and behavioural abnormality. Claim it if you wish, but you stand the risk of being labelled Obsessive/Neurotic unless it's a simple Allergy to cow's milk. Symptoms such as lip tingling, rash, vomiting, abdominal distension or BORBORYGMI will place your case on a firmer footing if your Doctor is enlightened. See GLUTEN-FREE DIET.

FORENSIC MEDICINE The branch of the profession that will examine your body if your demise is less than accidental or expected. See EPITAPH.

FOREIGN BODY Anything alien that penetrates an individual's body and causes a violent reaction. In the case of Spanish waiters, the violent reaction usually comes from the girl's father.

FORMICATION 1. Unpleasant sensation that one is crawling with ants. Common in the presence of Alcohol or other Drug Abuse. Also caused by some RASHES.
Tip: Before calling the Doctor, it's worth checking that you aren't actually crawling with ants.
2. Symptom which can lead to major complications if misheard over the telephone.

FRACTURE 1. An abnormal break in a bone, often caused by a fall.
2. An abnormal break in the erect penis due to a sudden change in velocity and direction. Requires urgent splinting with a tongue depressor or pencil until the urologist arrives. He will be delayed by stopping on the way to have a good laugh.
3. An abnormal breakdown of the Doctor-patient relationship, inevitable after the above.

FRECKLE A gold-brown pigmented patch that forms on

skin exposed to sunlight. Freckles are harmless, but each raises the possibility of a MALIGNANT MELANOMA. Astute Hypochondriacs regularly consult at least one dermatologist.

FRIGIDITY The inability to enjoy sexual intercourse. It is most commonly diagnosed by men in women who simply don't fancy them.

FROZEN SECTION A quick method of examining a BIOPSY for an instant Diagnosis. Traditionally used to decide whether a breast lump was BENIGN or MALIGNANT. Now rarely performed, except when a Pathologist's wife can't remember whether the joint at the bottom of the freezer is lamb or beef.

FULMINANT A medical word describing a problem which develops faster, more severely and in a more spectacular manner than ever before thought possible. As such, an aspiration for all Hypochondriacs.

FUNCTIONAL DISORDER A Diagnosis that will make every Hypochondriac grit his teeth. This innocent-sounding phrase is how Doctors communicate to each other that your problem exists solely inside your head and that nothing physical is wrong. Reply quite firmly 'I can assure you my problem is ORGANIC.'

FURUNCLE# Doctor-impressing word for a nasty Boil.

G

GABA Abbreviation for Gamma Aminobutyric Acid. A NEUROTRANSMITTER which passes messages from one brain cell to another – assuming, of course, that you've got at least two.

GALL-BLADDER A small, pear-shaped pouch found just beneath the liver. It is designed to store bile, but usually gets bored and makes Gallstones instead. Few Hypochondriacs still possess one. See CHOLECYSTECTOMY.

GANGLION A Cystic Swelling arising from the sheath of a tendon – e.g., in the wrist. A Ganglion is filled with a thick, glue-like material which was traditionally burst by a good whack from the family Bible. The decline of religious studies has coincided with a resurgence of Ganglion surgery.

GANSER'S SYNDROME The giving of stupid answers to sensible questions – e.g., replying five when asked what two times two makes. It can be a form of MALINGERING or an Hysterical Reaction to STRESS. When your Doctor asks, 'How are you?' avoid the temptation of replying 'Fine'. There is a very real danger that he might believe you.

GAS AND AIR Life-saving form of anaesthetic used during NATURAL CHILDBIRTH. Similar to laughing gas, though women in Labour don't often see the joke.

GASTRECTOMY Removal of the stomach. If a Doctor recommends this as a method of slimming, you can be sure you're dealing with a quack.

GASTROENTERITIS See VOMITING; CHOLERA; DIARRHOEA; MONTEZUMA'S REVENGE; THE SQUITTERS; THE RUNS; DELHI BELLY; DONER DISASTER; ROARING RINGBURNERS; COCOA PLOPS; etc., etc.

GASTROSCOPY Examination of your stomach by inserting a telescope on a stick. A form of armchair THEATRE.

GAUZE An absorbent, open-weave cotton fabric used to dress wounds. Highly recommended as an emergency strainer for crusty port.

GENDER BENDER Someone who bends the physical and cultural markers of biological sex by wearing adornments usually reserved for the other side. It's always best to tell your Doctor what sex you really are. Otherwise, you could get HRT when you were consulting him about Barber's Rash.

GENE Microscopic codes inherited from both parents that provide the blueprint for your development. These are also the bastards that make you age, grow wrinkly, develop Heart Disease or CANCER and generally dictate how much hair grows in your nose and ears. So, if anything goes wrong in your life, blame your parents!

GENERAL MEDICAL COUNCIL The statutory body that disciplines any Doctor who doesn't take your Hypochondria seriously. Cherish these guys – they're on your side.

GENERAL PARALYSIS OF THE INSANE 1. A late sign of infection with Syphilis. Very rare nowadays.
2. The collective term to describe a bunch of PSYCHIATRISTS after their annual medical dinner.

GENERAL PRACTICE Misnomer for the very specific skills

possessed by a family Doctor. As the GP holds every Hypochondriac's entry ticket to the NHS theme park, it's best to keep on his side. Call him out day and night for every slight cough, twinge or aberration to improve his self-esteem and counselling skills. Thereby lies the path to greater fulfilment – a REFERRAL and hopefully a DIAGNOSIS.

GENERIC DRUG A drug marketed under its official name as opposed to its patented brand name. Generics are usually cheaper drugs, but their quality has been called into question. A Hypochondriac should only accept a prescription for a brand-name drug – a phrase such as 'I don't want none of that there generic stuff' should do the trick.

GENE THERAPY 1. The Treatment of Disease by inserting a new Gene to replace a faulty one. The absolute frontier of scientific medicine.
2. A little-known American Country & Western singer.

GENETIC CODE The exact sequence in which GENES are aligned on the cell's nuclear street map. Only one Gene Complex is likely still to remain undetected by the year 2000 – but don't worry, it's the one that causes Hypochondria, so you'll be all right.

GENETIC FINGERPRINTING Analysing your Genetic Code to point the finger of blame. A popular device in crime novels written by people who know absolutely nothing about the subject.

GENITAL HERPES Unbelievably trivial problem that has been hyped out of all proportion. So you get tiny ulcers on your willy – big deal. Avoid intercourse when they're there and buy shares in Durex when they're gone. If cold sores come back again (yawn) chill out until Symptom-free. As a

Hypochondriac you'll want maximum mileage out of any ailment, but wearing a badge saying 'I've got Herpes Two' is taking things a bit far – and tends to do little for your social life.

GENITO-URINARY DISEASE Politically correct term for Clap. See VD.

GERM A popular term for any Microscopic Organism that causes Disease. Some patients develop a PHOBIA against Germs, and have an OBSESSIVE–COMPULSIVE need continuously to wash their hands, wear a mask or cover the carpet with tissue paper. You should have no truck with this behaviour. It is not true Hypochondria – just a one-way ticket to the Psychiatrist's chair.

GET WELL CARDS Your attitude to these is inevitably ambivalent. While the fact that you've received a Get Well Card means you've convinced at least one person you're authentically ill, the last thing you want to do is to follow the instructions on the card.

GIARDIA 1. An obscure, tropical infection of the BOWELS causing DIARRHOEA and foul FLATUS. If you've got loose bowels and have ever been south of the Channel Isles, insist on having your sievcd stools microscopically examined for parasites. Hypochondriacs who belong to the Campaign for Real Ale are advised to look for other causes of their foul Flatus.
2. A misprint that's bad even by the *Guardian*'s standards.

GIDDINESS A Symptom you should only resort to when creativity is at a low ebb. Ginger it up a bit by claiming that SICK SINUS SYNDROME, Aortic Stenosis or Complete Heart Block runs in your family. If that isn't rewarded by an instant

ECG, mention those funny PALPITATIONS and ask about the SIDE EFFECTS of prescription drugs.

GILLES DE LA TOURETTE SYNDROME Since fifty per cent of its victims have bouts of Coprolalia, during which indiscriminate foul language is used, this is the perfect disorder to give Hypochondriacs *carte blanche* to tell their Doctors exactly what they think of them.

GLAND* A group of specialised cells that make and release Hormones or Enzymes. Any medical Symptoms can be safely blamed on your Glands. Try, though, to be specific about which Gland – the Pineal is worth its weight in gold to the Hypochondriac, as no one really knows why it's there.

GLANDULAR FEVER Never, ever, claim you're suffering from this – it's instantly recognised as the 'Kissing Disease'. Always use its proper name: Infectious Mononucleosis. Though it sounds the ideal vague illness for the Hypochondriac, it can in fact be rather tiresome. Expect the Sore Throat, Fever, Tiredness and Swollen Glands to lay you low for at least a month. Many sufferers need six months' CONVALESCENCE and don't feel right after a year. This is far too long for the average Hypochondriac. After a month you want to be back in that surgery with a whole new set of Symptoms.

GLIOMA One of the commonest types of Brain Tumour. If you notice any HEADACHE, unsteadiness, numbness, dizziness, visual problems, weakness or jerkiness, you need a full Neurological Work-up. Once you've got yourself properly worked up, call the Doctor and tell him you know you've got a Brain Tumour. Don't revise your Diagnosis until you've had at least one Isotope Brain Scan, a CAT scan and an MRI.

GLOSSECTOMY Removal of all or part of the tongue. Very tempting for any Surgeon treating a Hypochondriac.

GLUCOCORTICOIDS The *crème de la crème* of drugs. If you collapse and your Doctor stuffs you full of HYDROCORTISONE, you know he's taking you seriously.

GLUE EAR An accumulation of Fluid and Mucus in the middle ear. Common cause of Deafness in kids. Insist on a Myringotomy (surgical hole in the eardrum) and the insertion of a Grommet to let the gunge drain away. (But do check first that no practical joker has been putting superglue in your balaclava.)

GLUTEN-FREE DIET This is a treatment for Coeliac Disease, or Gluten Enteropathy. Its sufferers are allergic to that part of wheat known as Gluten. Since Coeliac Disease manifests many of the Symptoms of Malnutrition, you don't actually want to have it, but there's nothing to stop you saying, 'Erm, excuse me, but there isn't any Gluten in this sauce, is there?' every time you sit down to a meal. This is a quick and painless way of establishing your credentials as a serious invalid.

GLYCERYL TRINITRATE A drug that rapidly dilates blood vessels in the heart, brain and elsewhere. An instant cure for ANGINA PECTORIS with the SIDE EFFECT of causing simultaneous HEADACHES and ERECTIONS, which can lead to marital discord.

GOUT An exquisitely painful Metabolic Disorder in which Uric Acid crystals are deposited in joints. If anyone suggests you've been drinking too much port, remind them this is a Disease caused by Abnormal Purine Metabolism. That should shut them up.

GRAVE'S DISEASE Not as serious as it sounds. An overactive

51

Goitre in which the Immune System makes Antibodies against the Thyroid Gland. Named after a Physician, not the final resting place of his failures.

GROIN STRAIN Pain and tenderness in the groin, frequently caused by overstretching a muscle whilst playing sport. As this could mean Osteoarthritis of the hip or an incipient Hernia, you must have a full examination. Don't be surprised if your Doctor asks you to drop your shorts and cough – unless you're a lady.

GROUP THERAPY A form of Psychotherapy in which everyone sits round in a circle and tells their innermost secrets; after which the PSYCHOTHERAPIST goes away and has a good laugh.

GROWTH Benign, friendly and laid-back word for CANCER, so far as Hypochondriacs are concerned. Actually, quite a lot of Growths are non-cancerous, but what Hypochondriac would ever believe that?

GUINEA PIG Becoming one of these is something all Hypochondriacs should bear in mind as a possible route to that new drug, new Treatment, dishy new Consultant etc. Make sure you are fully informed of all the things that could go wrong; invent a few more of your own (no problem there), then lie back and enjoy expanding the frontiers of science.

GUMBOIL This sounds better if you call it a Dental Abscess.

GYNAECOLOGIST A ladies' man. An appointment with one of these is an absolute must for all female Hypochondriacs to tick off at least once in their annual REFERRALS diary. And, incidentally, the story of the Gynaecologist who wallpapered his hall through the letterbox is believed to be apocryphal.

H

HAEMATEMESIS The medical term for Vomiting Blood. Digested blood resembles coffee grounds – but don't be confused if yours look like tea leaves. If you can *read* the tea leaves, you'll save your doctor the trouble of making the Diagnosis.

HAEMATOMA# Doctor-impressing word for a nasty Bruise.

HAEMOPHILIA A bleeding disorder due to lack of Clotting Factor VIII. Most sufferers are male, as this disorder is sex-linked. If you're male and bruise easily, this is a definite possibility. If you're female and bruise easily, don't get involved with a MEDICAL STUDENT.

HAEMOPTYSIS# Doctor-impressing term for Coughing up Blood. This requires urgent referral to a Chest Physician. You need an X-ray and a Bronchoscopy (telescope stuffed into the lungs) at the very least. If you're a professional sword-swallower, Haemoptysis could be nature's way of telling you it's time to stop.

HAEMORRHOIDECTOMY Surgical removal of Haemorrhoids. Avoid this op like the plague. Although it keeps you in hospital for a respectable ten days, your BOTTOM takes weeks to heal and hurts like crazy when you have a pooh. You'll be stuffed up to the eyeballs with laxatives, dunked in warm water to relax your stricken sphincter – and given Paracetamol for the pain. Heroin would be more appropriate. Haemorrhoidectomy also has the ultimate embarrassing

SIDE EFFECT: loss of Anal Sensation, which can stop you controlling the release of wind.

HALLUX VALGUS A Deformity of the big toe in which the joint at the base sticks out. This is a more impressive-sounding alternative to the plain Bunion.

HANGOVER An unpleasant condition occurring the morning after a night before. Headache, Nausea and Vertigo predominate – but these can also be Symptoms of MENINGITIS, Brain Tumour and an Infection of the inner ear (Labyrinthitis). Even if you did down a bottle of Scotch the previous night, don't make it easy for the Doctor by confessing – let him work it out by excluding nastier Diagnoses first.

HARLEQUIN SYNDROME Sudden, unilateral Flushing and Sweating due to heat, exercise or eating spicy food. One-sided Venous Dilation like this could be an early sign of something very rare. You might have a Phaeochromocytoma with simultaneous Nerve Damage down one side. Alternatively, you may just have been sitting side-on to the fire for too long.

HAY FEVER The popular and less impressive term for Seasonal Allergic Rhinitis. Upgrade your Diagnosis as soon as possible. And bless you.

HEADACHE One of the commonest types of Pain. Most Hypochondriacs reject the simple Tension Headache as being too boring, and come up with a more exciting and unusual variant – e.g., a Temporal Headache with Tenderness at the outer forehead region. If you mention that Temporal Arteritis runs in your family, you'll get an instant Blood Test and an urgent Neurological REFERRAL. If your Doctor suggests a Temporal Artery BIOPSY and massive doses of Steroids, ask him to wait for the results of the Blood Test first.

NB: Headache can be a sign of: Sinusitis, Toothache, Migraine, Drug SIDE EFFECTS, Osteoarthritis of the neck, High Blood Pressure, Head Injury, Brain Tumour, Meningitis, Temporal Arteritis, Increased Pressure inside the skull and Stroke. Unfortunately for the aspiring Hypochondriac, it's more often due just to Tension, Muscular Spasm, Hangover or having gone off your sexual partner. Still, you needn't tell your Doctor that.

HEALTH CENTRE Strange term for a medical surgery dealing almost exclusively in Ill Health.

HEART ARRHYTHMIA An Irregularity in the Heartbeat. See PALPITATIONS. Can be caused by excess intake of Caffeine or Alcohol, but might mean SICK SINUS SYNDROME, Rheumatic Heart Disease, an Overactive Thyroid or a myriad of other complaints. Don't leave the consulting room until your Doctor has promised:

A resting ECG
A twenty-four hour Heart Tracing
A battery of Blood Tests
A bed in Coronary Care as soon as one comes free
That new wonder drug you read about in the paper
A resident resuscitation team with a Defibrillator.

See MACHINE THAT GOES PING!

HEART ATTACK See ANGINA PECTORIS; CARDIAC NEUROSIS; CHEST PAIN; CORONARY THROMBOSIS; MYOCARDIAL INFARCTION.

HEARTSINK PATIENT Someone who walks (limps, hobbles, crawls) into a consulting room and causes the Doctor's

55

heart to sink. If your Doctor is always palming you off on the GP trainee, you almost certainly fit this category. Congratulations – you are a fully-fledged Hypochondriac.

HEART TRANSPLANT The ultimate operation to aim for. Your exclusivity will fall as the number of successful operations increases, but your celebrity status will never be equalled by Hypochondriacs of lesser aspirations.

HEIMLICH MANOEUVRE A First Aid Treatment to save a person who's choking due to an airway blocked with food. Put both fists in their stomach and squeeze their midriff violently. A useful technique to use whenever someone you dislike clears their throat. Jump up and whack them in the solar plexus before explaining innocently that you were only saving their life.

HEMIBALLISMUS 1. Uncontrollable flinging movements of the arm and leg on one side of the body, due to a brain disorder.
2. Swearword for use when trapping a TESTICLE in your zip.

HENOCH-SCHONLEIN PURPURA Inflammation of small blood vessels in which leaking blood causes a widespread, purple RASH. But who cares what it actually is – what a wonderful-sounding Disease to be able to say you've got!

HEPATITIS Serious Inflammation of the liver, causing JAUNDICE. If you turn yellow, especially in the whites of your eyes, contact a Doctor straight away. If you turn yellow but your eye whites stay crystal clear, lay off the carrots and stop using the cheap fake tan.

HERMAPHRODITISM A congenital disorder in which both male and female sex organs are present. Not actually as much fun as it sounds.

HICCUPS A sudden, involuntary contraction of the diaphragm. This causes the vocal cords to snap shut, producing a characteristic sound. As Hiccups are occasionally triggered by irritation of the Phrenic Nerves, Pleurisy, PNEUMONIA, a stomach TUMOUR, Pancreatitis, Alcoholism or HEPATITIS, your Doctor must take them seriously. They're also very useful for irritating people in the surgery WAITING ROOM.

HIGH, HOT AND A HELLUVA LOT The instructions a Surgeon gives a Nurse when planning your Diagnostic ENEMA.

HIPPOCRATIC OATH An oath, devised by the ancient Greek Physician Hippocrates, which is traditionally taken by Doctors when they qualify. It consists of seven pledges.

1. THAT THE DOCTOR WILL HOLD HIS OR HER TEACHERS AS DEAR AS HIS OR HER OWN PARENTS. (*Given the way many doctors behave towards their families, that's not saying much.*)
2. THAT HE OR SHE WILL IMPART HIS OR HER KNOWLEDGE (*assuming that he or she has got any*) ONLY TO HIS OR HER SONS, HIS OR HER TEACHER'S SONS AND RECOGNISED STUDENTS. (*Pretty unfair on his or her daughters, isn't it?*)
3. THAT HE OR SHE WILL TREAT HIS OR HER PATIENTS TO THE BEST OF HIS OR HER ABILITY AND JUDGEMENT. (*That's not saying much either, is it?*)
4. THAT HE OR SHE WILL LEAVE ALL SURGICAL OPERATIONS TO BE PERFORMED BY SURGEONS. (*Well, at least then the Doctor can't be blamed when things go wrong.*)
5. THAT HE OR SHE WILL NOT HAVE SEX WITH HIS OR HER PATIENTS. (*At least not while anyone's watching.*)
6. THAT HE OR SHE WILL NOT GIVE POISON AND NOT

GIVE A WOMAN A PESSARY TO PROCURE ABORTION
(*though presumably other methods are all right*).
7. THAT HE OR SHE WILL KEEP TO HIM- OR HERSELF ALL
INFORMATION. (*That's no great problem. As every
Hypochondriac knows to his or her cost, no Doctor ever
remembers anything about his or her case.*)

HORMONE 1. A chemical released into the blood stream by
one tissue that has an effect on another tissue somewhere
else in the body. Any Symptom can be blamed on Hormones
if you're scratching around for an explanation.
2. Noise of faked orgasm heard outside a brothel.

HORMONE REPLACEMENT THERAPY (HRT) No Meno-
pausal female Hypochondriac would be without this. If a
Doctor prescribes HRT for you, be grateful and start looking
for a toy boy. (If, on the other hand, he prescribes HGV,
have no further truck with him.)

HOUSE CALL A common occurrence in the days of Dr
Finlay. Now rarer. Hypochondriacs should keep a tally of the
number of these they manage to achieve in a year.

HOUSEMAID'S KNEE 1. Inflammation of the bursa, a
fluid-filled sac that overlies and cushions the kneecap. Usually due to prolonged kneeling.
2. A stabbing Pain in the groin experienced by lecherous
houseguests.

HYDROCORTISONE Vets give sick animals a shot of Hydrocortisone and ANTIBIOTIC then wait to see what happens. They
either get better or die. If only Doctors did the same, there'd be
a lot less competition for you from other Hypochondriacs.
Hydrocortisone is the panacea for all ills – smooth it on to
inflamed skin, anally retain it for Haemorrhoids, squirt it up

HIT LIST

A **hypochondriac's** Hit List contains all the specialists you aim to see in any one year [See **DIAGRAM**]. Tick them off according to success. Each tick counts as one point. A double hit for any speciality scores 3 - and a triple hit scores 5. A dedicated hypochondriac must obtain a score of at least 15 to maintain credibility.

Specialist
- Andrologist [for males]
- Anaesthetist
- Cardiac Surgeon
- Cardiologist
- Casualty Consultant
- Chest Physician
- Diabetologist
- Dermatologist
- Endocrinologist
- ENT Surgeon
- Gastroenterologist
- General Physician
- General Surgeon
- Generally Anybody
- Gerontologist [for over 65s]
- Gynaecologist [for females]
- Haematologist
- Neurologist
- Oncologist
- Ophthalmologist
- Orthopaedic Surgeon
- Paediatrician [for under 16s]
- Pathologist [for CADAVERS]
- Proctologist
- Radiologist
- Transplant Surgeon
- Sexologist
- Urologist
- Venereologist
- Witch Doctor [Well, you never know]

your nose for RHINITIS or eat it with ice-cream when you collapse. Well OK, it does have some SIDE EFFECTS, but a true Hypochondriac will just welcome the extra Symptoms.

HYPERGLYCAEMIA High Blood Sugar Level. This is a sign of DIABETES MELLITUS or occasionally of too many doughnuts. Sugar spills over into the urine, so the classic test is to dip your finger in urine and lick (ugh).

HYPERVENTILATION Over-breathing, especially during a PANIC ATTACK. This blows off carbon dioxide from the body, causing Low Blood Acidity, tingling round the mouth, tremor and dizzyness. Put a brown paper bag over your head and breathe deeply – this not only brings carbon dioxide back into your lungs but also generally improves your appearance.

HYPOCHONDRIA The mistaken Diagnosis by uncaring Doctors of genuine Symptoms.

HYPOCHONDRIASIS# Doctor-impressing word for HYPO-CHONDRIA. You can try it on Doctors in an attempt to get your Symptoms taken more seriously, but unfortunately most of them already know the word.

HYPOCHONDRIUM The area on each side of the upper abdomen, beneath the ribs. This is the most common site of non-specific Abdominal Pain – hence it was adopted to describe the SYNDROME of HYPOCHONDRIA.

I

IATROGENIC A useful word describing any illness caused by a Physician during medical treatment – e.g., drug SIDE EFFECTS, swabs left inside the belly, bones accidentally broken under Anaesthetic. An area ripe for MEDICO-LEGAL plundering. If your initial requests for investigation fall on stony ground, try suggesting that your Symptoms are Iatrogenic. REFERRAL sparks will immediately start to fly.

ICE PACKS Do-it-yourself treatment for sprains and strains. A bag of frozen peas does wonders for aching ankles. Inventive Hypochondriacs will ensure that Frostbite ensues.

ICHTHYOSIS Literally, fish-skin Disease. A rare condition in which the skin is scaly, dry, thick and dark due to abnormal production of the protein keratin. A female Hypochondriac who experiences this condition below the waist only should not rule out the possibility that she has turned into a mermaid.

ICTERUS# Doctor-impressing word for Yellow Jaundice.

IDIOPATHIC Super word for the Hypochondriac, meaning 'of unknown cause'. All you have to do is say your— (fill in desired Symptom) is due to an Idiopathic, IATROGENIC SYNDROME, and you'll have convinced even your Doctor that something serious is wrong. This approach also carries the pleasing implication of a distinct failure on the part of the medical profession to come up with a proper Diagnosis.

IMAGINATION In the true Hypochondriac, the most highly developed special sense.

IMMUNE SYSTEM The part of the body that fights invasion from Micro-organisms, transplanted tissues, CANCER cells and anything 'foreign'.

IMMUNE SYSTEM DYSFUNCTION* The Hypochondriac's best friend. Any Symptom may safely be blamed on this. Auto-immune Diseases – where the body attacks itself – are very much in vogue.

IMMUNOGLOBULIN Not, as many believe, a character from Tolkien. In fact an unbelievably complicated word for an Antibody.

IMPETIGO A highly contagious Bacterial Skin Infection. Classic LESIONS start as small, fluid-filled Blisters which weep and produce a golden crust. Spread is rapid, and ANTIBIOTIC tablets or creams are needed. As this Infection is so easily transmissible, a good Hypochondriac will protect himself and others by staying indoors for weeks and regularly calling out the Doctor.

IMPLANT Any material, natural or synthetic, that is inserted and retained for a medical purpose – e.g.:

> Breast Implant
> Hormonal Implant
> Artificial Hip Joint
> Heart Pacemaker
> False Eye
> Arterial By-pass Graft
> Sperm during ARTIFICIAL INSEMINATION
> Pair of Forceps mislaid during operation.

IMPOTENCE The inability of a male to achieve or maintain an ERECTION long enough (in every sense of the word) to satisfy his partner. With the female sex becoming increasingly demanding and the male sex becoming increasingly self-questioning, the INCIDENCE of this common Disease is bound to go up, so to speak. Sex is obviously a fruitful area for the male Hypochondriac, though it should be pointed out that the chances of getting referred to a really dishy surrogate partner, who then becomes obsessed by your virility and falls madly in love with you, are minimal.

IMPOTENCE, REMEDIES FOR These have a history as old as time. As a general rule, avoid remedies which involve the Implantation of Telescopes, Inflation with Helium, or any hydraulic equipment bigger than you are (girls tend to notice when you take it with you to a disco).

INCIDENCE A measure of how common a Disease is, measured as the number of new cases diagnosed over a given period – e.g., the incidence of Hypochondria is around 999 per 1000 people per year. The odd one is you, because while all the others are just making up their Symptoms, you know that yours are absolutely real.

INCISION The invasion of your body by the Surgeon's knife. An experienced Hypochondriac's skin should be a road map of scar tissue. For types of Incision, see diagram.

INCUBATION PERIOD The time-lapse between Infection and the appearance of the first signs of a Disease. This is a gift to a Hypochondriac. Since Symptoms take time to appear, it is possible to spend your entire life in a panic about the possibility that you've just been infected even though there's nothing to show yet.

TYPES OF INCISION

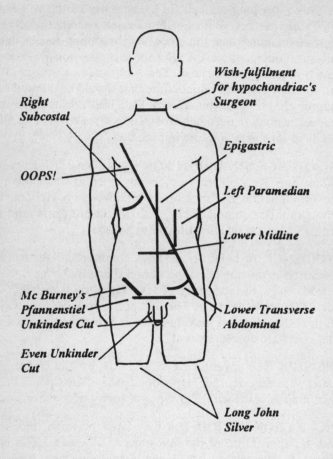

Wish-fulfilment
for hypochondriac's
Surgeon

Right
Subcostal

Epigastric

OOPS!

Left Paramedian

Lower Midline

Mc Burney's
Pfannenstiel
Unkindest Cut

Lower Transverse
Abdominal

Even Unkinder
Cut

Long John
Silver

INDIGESTION A catch-all phrase for a variety of Symptoms brought on by eating. Try to avoid the word if you can – it's a Symptom that switches Doctors right off. Go instead for Gastritis, Peptic Ulcers, Helicobacter, or Cholecystitis. You may not convince your GP, but think how it'll help the next time you play Scrabble.

INFARCTION# Doctor-impressing word for Tissue Death due to lack of blood supply and oxygen. So, if you find you've got some Dead Tissues, please place them in the receptacle provided.

INFLUENZA A viral Disease that attacks the respiratory system. Hypochondriacs have several attacks of this in any one year, at times when lesser mortals only manage a COMMON COLD.

INGROWING TOENAIL A tendency for the big toenails to dig into the tender, surrounding flesh. As this could lead to Cellulitis, SEPTICAEMIA, Gangrene or even Amputation of the foot, for a Hypochondriac the first twinge in the big toe necessitates urgent medical attention, crutches and installation of a chair-lift.

INOPERABLE Any medical condition that cannot be alleviated or cured by surgery. The ultimate Inoperable Condition is of course Hypochondria.

INSOMNIA Difficulty in sleeping. Insomnia makes Doctors yawn, so in the surgery talk about DEPRESSION instead.

INSULIN A hormone produced by the pancreas GLAND, of which too little causes DIABETES MELLITUS. This has interesting possibilities – fat Hypochondriacs can blame their obesity on Insulin Hypersensitivity, whilst stressed-out, overweight businessmen with High Blood Pressure can blame Insulin Resistance.

INSURANCE, MEDICAL Essential safety-net for the serious Hypochondriac. But don't be too optimistic about getting a no-claims bonus. Incidentally, Medical Insurance should not be confused with an Insurance Medical, something that has to be undergone when taking out an insurance policy, getting a mortgage, or marrying into a rich and suspicious family. Insurance Medicals are very popular with GPs, whom they provide with a nice little fee for doing very little.

INTENSIVE CARE The Hypochondriac's Mecca. Go for it every time. The constant screening, wires, strings, gizmos and MACHINES THAT GO PING! make everything else worthwhile. The fact that your friends have to put on masks and robes to visit you will convince them that you really are ill.

INTERCURRENT A Disease that occurs during the course of another existing Disease is said to be 'Intercurrent'. Though this obviously offers great scope to the inventive Hypochondriac, it should be mentioned that Doctors tend to be sceptical if the Intercurrent Diseases complained of exceed two.

INTRACTABLE Any condition that does not respond to treatment and goes on for some time. Applies to all Hypochondriac complaints.

IRRITABLE BOWEL SYNDROME* This is a good one. Since its Symptoms range from watery DIARRHOEA to long-lasting CONSTIPATION, there's something here to fit every kind of digestive abnormality. Its causes may be related to STRESS, or DIET, or ANXIETY or DEPRESSION . . .

or anything you feel like, really. Go to your doctor with the full set of three: Irritable Bowel Syndrome, Grumbling Appendix and your own natural Bad Temper – and you'll be able to moan on at him for hours.

ITCHING An inevitable sign of something nasty. If, on inspection, your doctor backs off, then it's definitely the time to worry.

'IT'S ALL RIGHT – I'M A DOCTOR' Justification for behaviour which would lead to most people outside the medical profession being locked up.

IWTBIBNTI SYNDROME Common among Hypochondriacs who finally get a Diagnosis of something really LIFE-THREATENING, like CANCER or MENINGITIS. The initials stand for: 'I Wanted To Be Ill, But Not *That* Ill.'

J

JAUNDICE Turning yellow due to a build-up of Bilirubin, a waste product. May be due to:

LIVER Disease – e.g., HEPATITIS, Liver Failure breaking down too many blood cells
Blockage of the bile duct – e.g., Gallstones, TUMOUR.

Yellowness in which the whites of the eyes stay white can be produced by eating too many carrots. Gives the naming of Bugs Bunny a whole new meaning.

JEJUNAL BIOPSY A TEST in which a Doctor goes fishing for a bit of your insides. Basically, you swallow the equivalent of a razor blade tied to a piece of string. When it's in the right place, he gives a yank and activates the blade. Your BIOPSY is then fished out by reeling in the string. Rumours of accidental VASECTOMY or CIRCUMCISION by Jejunal Biopsy have not been substantiated.

JOGGER'S NIPPLE Soreness of the nipple due to rubbing against clothes. Can be prevented by rubbing with PETROLEUM JELLY. As this condition can be an early Symptom of Paget's Disease of the Nipple (a form of CANCER) or of Cellulitis or breast ABSCESS, have it checked out straight away.
Tip: Tell your Doctor about the Petroleum Jelly.

JOGGING A method of keeping fit, so clearly of no interest to Hypochondriacs.

JOURNALS, MEDICAL All Hypochondriacs should subscribe to as many of these as possible. Nothing infuriates a hard-pressed GP more than having in his surgery a patient who knows more about state-of-the-art medicine than he does.

JUGULAR VEIN Part of the anatomy to aim for when the Consultant claims you do not have an ORGANIC disease.

K

KERATOACANTHOMA Not, as it sounds, the name of a beach on Corfu, but a bizarre Skin Nodule that initially develops as a small Wart and rapidly grows in size to reach about 2cm across. The sides bulge and the centre looks white. If left alone, it will slowly disappear, usually leaving a pit. Most people prefer to have them surgically removed – after all, how do you know it's not cancerous?

KETOSIS A serious condition in which Ketones build up in the body. These result when fats are burned during a severe lack of glucose – e.g. Starvation, Fasting. Ketones cause Nausea, Abdominal Pain and if untreated, lead to Confusion and even DEATH. So if you've missed lunch and feel light-headed or sick, rush to the surgery and have your urine tested for Ketosis.

KEYHOLE SURGERY The art of performing invasive procedures using tiny incisions. Telescopes and cutting instruments are poked through to explore and, in many cases, excavate the secret recesses of your body. This technique allows an operation to be performed as a day case without admission to hospital. Sod that for a lark – a Hypochondriac needs at least two good overnight stays to achieve maximum sympathy points.

KIDNEY* The Kidneys make urine and a good accompaniment for steak pies. Vague claims of kidney problems are always taken seriously – Kidney Failure is LIFE-THREATENING, and may need treatment with Dialysis or a

Kidney TRANSPLANT. If you notice any problems with your WATERWORKS, if your ankles swell up or you get puffy under the eyes, always ask for a check-up. If you notice blood in your urine, start running and don't stop until you reach the surgery.

KIDNEY FUNCTION TESTS A battery of Blood and Urinary Tests which will be triggered by your arriving breathless in the surgery after the above. Now is not the time to get squeamish and find it difficult to pee whilst several people are watching.

KILOCALORIE Those innocuous little units, of which there are only five in every peanut, that creep up on you and result in excess flab. The bastards.

KLUMPKE'S PARALYSIS 1. Paralysis and wasting of the lower arm and hand caused by injury to the First Thoracic Nerve – usually by a dislocated shoulder.
2. An excuse worth trying on your boss when you arrive late in the office. 'Sorry, last night I had an attack of Klumpke's Paralysis.' Mind you, he'll probably guess you were just drunk.

KOILONYCHIA# An impressive word that describes fingernails shaped like spoons. May be due to Iron Deficiency Anaemia – or interesting genes. Jolly useful for eating yoghurt at a picnic when the cutlery's been forgotten, though.

KOPLIK'S SPOTS White spots on the inner cheek that herald the onset of MEASLES. Classically, they resemble grains of salt on a red velvet cushion (rather poetic image, that). Once the RASH appears, Koplik's Spots depart. It's worth checking inside your mouth every day – after all,

Measles is a notifiable disease, and if you get it, Mrs Bottomley wants to be told right away.

KORSAKOFF'S SYNDROME A deterioration of brain and nerves, which leads to pathological lying. Some authorities maintain that it is caused by Vitamin Deficiency brought on by excessive drinking; others claim it is brought on by excessive drinking full stop.

KURU A progressive Brain Disease found in New Guinea, caused by a Slow Virus that's spread by Cannibalism. If you've recently eaten any hamburgers or given any love-bites and feel a bit odd, it's worth considering the possibility. It's also a useful one because your doctor probably won't have heard of it.

KYPHOSIS An excessive curvature of the spine. To check for this, take off your clothes and stand sideways, nude, in front of a mirror. Make sure the window cleaner's gone first.

L

LABOUR 1. Childbirth, the hardest work any woman will have to do.
2. This was once a political party.

LACTATION The Production and Secretion of milk. Usually signifies recent Childbirth. If you Lactate and have not been Pregnant:

A) Rush to the Doctor for an instant Prolactin Hormone Test

B) Ask your partner to stop stimulating your nipples quite so assiduously.

LAPAROSCOPY The insertion of a telescope into the abdominal cavity to inspect the Pelvic Organs, GALL-BLADDER, APPENDIX or LIVER. Many a female Hypochondriac has been sterilised via this route. A few now have their Gall-bladders removed through a hole so tiny the organ has to be talked out. See KEYHOLE SURGERY.

LAPAROTOMY The precursor of the above procedure. This operation calls for a whacking great incision across the abdomen. The Surgeon then plunges in with both hands and has a good feel around, which invariably fails to elucidate your problem. Whereupon the Surgeon climbs in with both feet and has a good saunter round before declaring nothing wrong. This doesn't, however, stop him removing your APPENDIX or GALL-BLADDER to appease the ADMINISTRATOR. So weigh yourself before and after the op to see how much is missing.

LARYNGITIS Inflammation of the larynx. Never admit to a mere SORE THROAT, always go husky and claim this one.

LARYNGOTRACHEOBRONCHITIS An even better alternative to the common SORE THROAT. If you can cough, splutter and look pale whilst suffering from LARYNGITIS, this is the one to go for. If you can spit a little Phlegm, all the better. In fact, for a Hypochondriac, the only disadvantage of this complaint is pronouncing it.

LASER An instrument that produces a concentrated beam of Light Amplification by Stimulated Emission of Radiation. Laser beams have many uses in medicine, including cutting, coagulation or destruction of unwanted tissues. All Hypochondriacs should aim for at least one Laser Treatment per decade – even if you have to pay for it. It looks good on your Medical Notes.

LASSA FEVER The ultimate Yuppy Flu – a dangerous African Viral Infection acquired by inhaling tropical rat's urine. Why anyone would want to inhale tropical rat's urine is beyond belief. If you get Lassa Fever you'll find that all medical, nursing and ambulance personnel you meet will be wearing asbestos moon suits, deep-sea diving equipment and ten layers of sanitised rubber – which maybe'll give you a clue about how infectious they think you are.

LEFT ILIAC FOSSA The bottom left-hand corner of the abdomen. Try to avoid a Pain here – your Doctor is unlikely to take much notice. It usually only signifies CONSTIPATION or a twinge of Diverticular Disease. Better to have your Pain in the Right Iliac Fossa, where it could easily mean APPENDICITIS.

LEGIONNAIRE'S DISEASE 1. A type of PNEUMONIA

caused by a bug that inhabits air-conditioning and water systems.

2. A disorder characterised by the desire to forget and the affectation of a handkerchief at the back of your hat.

LENTIGO# Doctor-impressing word for a freckle-like brown spot that appears on the skin with advancing age. Granny probably calls them Liver Spots. As you can't be sure they're not a rare form of MALIGNANT MELANOMA, wheel out your pet Dermatologist for a spot diagnosis.

LEPTOSPIROSIS A rare disease caused by a bacterium excreted in rat's urine. Fever, Chills, Headache, Rashes and sometimes JAUNDICE develop after an INCUBATION PERIOD of one to three weeks. Often develops in people foolish enough to bathe in dirty rivers full of rat's urine. If you do become unwell after a boating picnic, bear this one firmly in mind – you want ANTIBIOTICS sooner rather than later. If you have the habit of inhaling while on boating picnics, see LASSA FEVER.

LESION Catch-all word for any abnormal Spot, Blemish, Wound, Infection, TUMOUR, ABSCESS or FRECKLE. A useful word to bandy around, as in 'I've got this Lesion,' or 'My Lesion's the biggest the Doctor's ever seen.' But if you do it too often, people are likely to say, 'Why don't you go off and join the Foreign Lesion!'

LIFE EXPECTANCY The number of years a person can expect to live. Hypochondriacs expect very little, though many continue whingeing away to their Doctors well into their nineties.

LIFE-THREATENING This describes the *crème de la crème* of Symptoms which, if ignored any longer, will result in your ultimate demise. True Hypochondriacs will take great care in choosing the place where and the Physician to whom they demonstrate Life-Threatening Symptoms. The aim is to brush lightly with eternity before being scooped back by the MACHINE THAT GOES PING!

LIGATION The art of tying up in knots. Surgeons ligate blood vessels and ducts before cutting them (just pray that they cut the right side of the knot). See LITIGATION.

LITIGATION The art of tying up in legal knots, especially of a Surgeon whose surgical LIGATION has failed.

LISTERIOSIS A fashionable Infection caught from eating undercooked meat and unpasteurised dairy products. Since most Hypochondriacs have eaten meat or cheese within the last twenty-four hours, it's always a viable Disease to complain of.

LITHOTOMY POSITION The ultimate embarrassment, in which you sit on a high chair, or lie on a bed, and open your legs for all you're worth. Your ankles are then grabbed and tucked up into some overhanging STIRRUPS, leaving your tail-end open to all four winds. It's brilliant for the Doctor, who can poke his nose in where you'd rather it wasn't poked – but not so good for you. Try getting out of this by claiming you have an Easily Dislocatable hip. If that fails, ask for a brown paper bag and put it over your head.

LOBOTOMY An OPERATION to sever the Frontal Lobe of the brain. This is the method, now proved to be ineffective, of treating depressed patients by making cuts in specified areas. Not to be confused with La Bottomley, a woman who uses the method, now proved to be ineffective, of treating depressed patients by making cuts in specified areas.

LOCUM A temporary relief Doctor who will want to hear your entire medical history from start to finish. If you have the opportunity to see a Locum, always take it. For one thing, he probably won't be aware of your history of Hypochondria. And for another, it's a wonderful chance of a free SECOND OPINION.

LUDWIG'S ANGINA A rare bacterial infection of the mouth that becomes LIFE-THREATENING as it spreads to the throat. If not treated immediately, swelling interferes with BREATHING. A good suggestion to make to your Doctor when you turn up in the surgery with a SORE THROAT – oops, sorry, LARYNGOTRACHEOBRONCHITIS.

LUMBAGO A catch-all phrase for Low Back Pain. Reject any attempt by your Doctor to label your Symptoms as Lumbago. At the very least go for Prolapsed Intervertebral Disc.

LUMPECTOMY Highly technical word meaning removal of a Lump. See – ECTOMY.

LYME DISEASE A bacterial Disease transmitted by tick bites. A red dot appears at the site of the bite (see LESION) which expands to a diameter of half a centimetre. This is accompanied by FEVER, HEADACHE, and Muscular Aches and Pains. Almost any Symptom can be attributed to Lyme Disease, especially if you've ever walked on a moor, or cuddled a sheep (see FETISHISM).

M

MACHINE THAT GOES PING! Any highly technical piece of wizardry that goes Ping! Ping! Ping! usually in time with your pulse. Rumour has it that Machines That Go Ping! are only switched on in television hospital series or when an ADMINISTRATOR is around.

'MAD COW' DISEASE 1. Bovine Spongiform Encephalopathy, or BSE.
2. Something that afflicts NURSES when they become WARD SISTERS.

MAGNETIC RESONANCE IMAGING (MRI) State-of-the-art diagnostic technique using mirrors, magnets and magic. The ultimate TEST to get under your belt. Don't leave hospital without it.

MALAISE A vague feeling of being unwell, which as a general Symptom doesn't give the Doctor much of a clue. Needless to say, all Hypochondriacs suffer from this at all times.

MALFORMATION Any Deformity, especially one that's Congenital. It's worth knowing that:

A HEADACHE could be due to a Vascular Malformation within the skull.
Hypochondria could be due to a Congenital Malformation of the brain. You see, it's not really your fault, despite what the doctor may say.

MALIGNANT A term used to describe a nasty condition

that gets progressively worse, leading to DEATH. All Hypochondriacs' Symptoms are automatically Malignant until
proved otherwise.

MALIGNANT MELANOMA* A serious form of skin CAN-
CER characterised by a skin LESION which grows larger,
becomes blacker, itches, scabs or starts to bleed. In the mind
of the dedicated Hypochondriac, any FRECKLE, Mole,
WART, Felt Pen Mark or speck of Mascara is potentially one
of these.

MALINGERING The deliberate falsifying of Symptoms to
obtain time off work, avoid military service, or obtain
compensation. It is important to distinguish Malingering
from HYPOCHONDRIASIS. Malingerers *pretend* to be ill;
Hypochondriacs *know* they're ill.

MANIA Extreme Mental Disorder with overactivity, elation
and irritability. Common amongst fans of Tom Cruise and
Take That. See PSYCHOSIS.

MANIC-DEPRESSIVE DISORDER A psychiatric disturbance in which life's highs are more than balanced by the
lows. Grandiose aspirations are wiped out by total negativity
in baffling mood swings. Hypochondriacs whose hopes are
raised by a Diagnosis of something serious that later turns
out to be utterly trivial know exactly how this feels.

MASOCHISM Marriage to a Hypochondriac.

MASTURBATION Sexual self-stimulation frequently accompanied by vivid erotic fantasies. Ninety per cent of males and
sixty-five per cent of females indulge on a regular basis.
When asked why they prefer it to sexual activity with a
partner, twelve per cent of men said it was because during
Masturbation they met a better class of person.

MASTURBATION, EXCESSIVE Although this won't, as the Victorians believed, grow hairs on your palm, impair your eyesight or turn you mad, it is still possible to overindulge. As a general rule, if anything actually drops off, give it a rest for a day or two.

ME See MYALGIC ENCEPHALOMYELITIS.

MEASLES A Viral Illness with an INCUBATION PERIOD of eight to fourteen days. Symptoms start with a FEVER, runny nose, sore eyes and cough. A few days later, the classic RASH of red Macules appears, which form a giant join-the-dots game. Sadly, victims are usually too unwell to play.

MEATUS A canal or passageway in the body. The best known is the External Auditory Meatus – the ear hole. Be careful about using this word – most doctors seem to have forgotten it. Phrases such as 'I've got this problem with my back Meatus,' or 'There's this Discharge coming from my front Meatus' usually receive a blank stare and a fumble towards your ear lobes.

NB: The word is pronounced 'Mee-ay-tus'. Bear this in mind to avoid misunderstandings when somebody says, 'Meet us round the back'.

MEDICAL DICTIONARY The Hypochondriac's bible.

MEDICAL NOTES The Hypochondriac's CV.

MEDICAL RESEARCH The branch of medicine that has run out of rats and guinea pigs and has taken to practising on Hypochondriacs instead.

MEDICAL STUDENTS Embryo Doctors who approach the accumulated learning of centuries with the sniggering humour of five-year-olds.

MEDICATION Any DRUG, PLACEBO, Tablet, Capsule, Syrup, Elixir, Liquid, Injection, Suppository, Douche, ENEMA or Horse Pill prescribed by a Doctor to treat a Disease. Make sure you take them as prescribed, in the right order, the right number of times – and through the right orifice. The Doctor cannot be held responsible if you swallow the Suppository, gargle with the Douche, or try to stick the Injection up your bottom – even if that's what he'd dearly have loved to tell you to do with it.

MEDICINE, PRIVATE A branch of medicine where carpets are plush, paintings Old Masters, receptionists polite and Doctors obsequious to the point of nauseation. If you can afford it, or have conned your employer into paying for it, this is the one for you. Each and every Symptom will be explored, prodded and investigated until the bill has stretched to several thousand pounds. Once the Consultant has saved up enough for his next Bentley, he may suddenly find you less interesting. As soon as he's decided he really needs a yacht, however, the fascination with your case will mysteriously return.

MEDICO-LEGAL COMPENSATION Damages received for an injury resulting from medical negligence or malpractice. In reality, claims for Compensation reduce the Hypochondriac to a gibbering wreck and the Doctor to the brink of suicide. As usual, the only one who profits from the case is the lawyer.

MEGALOBLAST Underdeveloped red corpuscles evident in certain forms of Anaemia. Also, incidentally, a very good name for a computer game.

MELANCHOLIA Blue mood derived from the Greek for 'black bile'. Now known as DEPRESSION, which sounds much less attractive. Don't tell your doctor you have Melancholia – you'll simply be advised to take two Aspirin and to stop watching *Brookside*.

MEMBRANE A thin layer of tissue that lines a body surface or forms a barrier, e.g., Peritoneum, Tympanic Membrane, Hymen, Meninges. These can become inflamed, e.g., Peritonitis, Meningitis. Although it's rare to have a case of Hymenitis, female Hypochondriacs might like to claim this as the cause of their lost virginity.

MENINGES The three MEMBRANES that get inflamed during MENINGITIS. If you want to impress your Doctor, they're called the Dura Mater (hard mother), Arachnoid (spidery one) and the Pia Mater (dutiful mother), all soaking in a bath of cerebrospinal fluid.

MENINGITIS Inflammation of the MENINGES. This Disease is the second commonest terror of all Hypochondriacs, beaten only by their fear of CANCER. Most Hypochondriacs will suspect Meningitis at least once a year – usually when a Coryza or Tension Headache is setting in.

MENOPAUSE Though this sounds as if it should mean sudden loss of male partners – and indeed that can be a SIDE EFFECT – the word in fact describes the cessation of MENSTRUATION. This is a wonderful time for the female Hypochondriac, justifying an endless round of: Hot Flushes, Night Sweats, Sleep Disturbance, Irritability, Tearfulness, ANXIETY, Poor Memory and Loss of Libido. Never mind, just swallow the HRT and you'll instantly feel one hundred per cent better – though of course you won't tell anyone that.

MENOPAUSE, MALE Men do not escape unscathed; they

may not stop menstruating, but the Male Menopause is a recognised condition. Symptoms to watch out for include sudden lust after unsuitably young women, purchase of Porsche, affectation of bomber jacket and exotic variegation of ties.

MENSTRUATION* The monthly shedding of the lining of the womb that someone, somewhere, thought funny enough to foist on women. As tax is payable on sanitary protection, it seems reasonable to assume that someone was the VAT man. Female Hypochondriacs should make it a point of honour that their Menstruation is abnormal. GPs just love that opening gambit: 'Doctor, it's my periods.'

METABOLISM* The all-encompassing term for every chemical reaction occurring within your body. Metabolism can be blamed for most problems if you're ever stuck for a scapegoat. To be ahead of the opposition, suggest an Inborn Error of Metabolism – an inherited defect of body chemistry of which at least 200 types are known. Choose a number – 301, say – and very few Doctors will be any the wiser. You can then fill in the Symptoms of your choice – and, with a bit of luck, invent an eponymous SYNDROME. (The ambition of every Hypochondriac is actually to have a disease named after them – why should that fellow Munchausen have it all his own way?)

METASTASIS A Secondary Tumour that has spread from a Primary CANCER at a distant site. Mutter 'SECONDARIES' and you will have the sympathy of every Doctor and hard-hearted Surgeon in the land. (Of course you won't get the sympathy of other Hypochondriacs, because they're not interested in anyone else's Symptoms – except to give them new ideas for their own.)

MICROSURGERY Surgical technique for performing delicate stitches using magnification and very steady hands. Used to sew back miscellaneous body parts after accidental amputation and also to reverse VASECTOMY. Nowadays success rates in Microsurgery are very high, so long as the severed body part is properly preserved. A man whose little finger was accidentally amputated in a supermarket had it perfectly sewn back in place, thanks to the quick wits of a checkout girl who put the digit into a tub of vanilla ice-cream. And in fact, so high were the standards of hygiene in the operation that afterwards the tub was returned to the supermarket shelf – as raspberry ripple.

MICTURITION# Doctor-impressing word for having a pee.

MID-LIFE CRISIS A mental wobbly which, for Hypochondriacs, bridges that awkward gap between Adolescence and Senility.

MIGRAINE A severe HEADACHE that unfortunately receives little in the way of sympathy. Shrug off advice about rest, dark, avoiding cheese and red wine, chocolate, etc. Insist on a Neurological Work-up, several scans and at least one serious attempt at diagnosing a Brain TUMOUR.

MILIARIA# Doctor-impressing word for Prickly Heat.

MINERAL DEFICIENCY* At least twenty Minerals are essential for health, and most Symptoms can be blamed on a Deficiency in one or other of them. Try the following Deficiencies for the following Symptoms:

Poor Taste – lack of Zinc (and breeding)
Anaemia – lack of Iron

Weakness – lack of Potassium
Almost anything – SELENIUM DEFICIENCY.

To effect a cure, take a Mineral supplement and wait for improvements.

NB: If you hear a clanging sound from inside your stomach, then you're probably exceeding the stated dose.

MITTELSCHMERTZ# Doctor-impressing word to describe Mid-Cycle Ovulation pain. If you're trying for a baby, now is the time for a quick bonk.

MONORCHISM The presence of only one TESTICLE. Tough luck, unless you're a woman, in which case – look on the bright side, it could be worse. See HEMIBALLISMUS.

MORBIDITY The state of being diseased. Advanced practitioners of HYPOCHONDRIASIS should adopt this little concept – and upgrade to Morbid Hypochondriacs.

MORNING-AFTER PILL Useful Prophylactic for the morning after a night before. This is actually more versatile than it sounds; it can be taken up to seventy-two hours after unprotected sex to remove that little twinkle from your eye. Read the instructions carefully – in spite of the name, it doesn't work for Hangovers.

MORNING SICKNESS Inappropriately named badge of office for Pregnancy. There's nothing to stop Nausea and VOMITING occurring twenty-four hours a day – that's a cheerful thought for the female Hypochondriac.

MORTALITY The death rate per 100,000 population per year, according to cause. One day, despite all your suffering, you'll end up a mere statistic. One hundred per cent of

Hypochondriacs will eventually die, but the fun lies in choosing the Disease, method and complexity involved in that Death.

MULTIPLE PERSONALITY A rare disorder in which a person has at least two distinct personalities which are usually very different. Hypochondriacs tend to have at least two basic personalities – the depressed one who can't convince other people there's anything wrong; and the one that becomes instantly cheerful when presented with a Diagnosis.

MUNCHAUSEN'S SYNDROME The art of taking HYPO-CHONDRIASIS that little bit too far. Also known as Hospital Addiction Syndrome, or Hospital Hobo. Sufferers complain of fictitious Symptoms that are pretended or self-induced. Munchers are not actually MALINGERING – they just love being patients and acting as dummies for trainee Surgeons. Unfortunately, these buggers give common or garden HYPO-CHONDRIASIS a bad name. You've got to admire them, however – one woman ran up hospital bills of £250,000 over twenty-five years. She had ten volumes of notes distributed between four hospitals and when found out, was under the care of ten Consultants, taking fifteen drugs. Altogether, she had wangled seventy-seven hospital admissions, eleven operations and spent a total of 856 days as an in-patient. Now there's a challenge for you.

MURMUR 1. A Heart Sound due to the abnormal, turbulent flow of blood. If you have one of these, you're virtually guaranteed regular trips to a Cardiologist for life.
2. Mutterings of disbelief or dissent when you lay all your Symptoms on the table, and the Consultant tosses them back without so much as a second glance.

MUTATION A permanent change in the genetic code –

some for the better, some for the worst. Many inherited Diseases are due to Mutations – e.g., HAEMOPHILIA; HYPO-CHONDRIASIS. Take any Mutation as a sign of exclusivity; your problems are bound to be different from anyone else's. No wonder the medical profession is baffled. You never know, you might achieve that Holy Grail of all Hypochondriacs – having a Disease or Syndrome named after you.

MYALGIA# Doctor-impressing word for Muscular Pains.

MYALGIC ENCEPHALOMYELITIS A trendy disorder, usually shortened to ME. Also known as Post-Viral Fatigue Syndrome, Iceland Disease, Epidemic Neuromyasthenia and Royal Free Disease. Take your pick of these when reporting at the surgery, but try not to use ME. The latter is now synonymous with the rude term 'Yuppy Flu', and only a very enlightened Doctor will take you seriously. Request a MAGNETIC RESONANCE IMAGING scan and an appointment with a top NEUROLOGIST. One further down the pack just simply won't do.

MYOCARDIAL INFARCTION (MI)# Doctor-impressing term for a Heart Attack, or Coronary Thrombosis. Any Chest Pain, especially if it's tight (like a bear hug), comes on suddenly, is situated behind the sternum and radiates into your left arm or up the side of your jaw, is an MI until proven otherwise. Dial 999 and get yourself into Coronary Care as soon as you can. Request treatment with a Clot Buster and enjoy the IATROGENIC SIDE EFFECTS whilst this wonder drug saves your life.

MYOCARDIAL INFARCTION, SILENT One of the above, but without any Pain. This is good news for Hypochondriacs, giving them the perfect excuse to suspect a Silent MI whenever they feel like it, regardless of whether or not they've got any Symptoms. Silent MIs are especially common after retirement age, but that shouldn't stop you worrying from your late teens onwards – especially if you're male and Coronaries run in your family.

MY Personal pronoun beloved of Hypochondriacs. They never speak about *the* Doctor, Consultant, Surgeon, Oncologist, Proctologist, etc., but always *my* Doctor, Consultant, Surgeon, Oncologist, Proctologist, etc. 'My operation' is the cue for at least half an hour of blow-by-blow action replay from any Hypochondriac who has managed to get under the Surgeon's knife.

MYSTERY, MEDICAL How all Hypochondriacs would love to be labelled. 'I'm a medical mystery, me' is a phrase commonly heard at Hypochondriacal conventions.

N

NARCOPLEPSY A sleep disorder with excessive, CHRONIC daytime Drowsiness. Victims tend to fall asleep several times per day. Attacks last from a few seconds to several hours. Cataplexy – sudden loss of muscle tone without loss of consciousness – also occurs, making you flop gracefully to the floor like a sack of lumpy potatoes. If this happens to you in the consulting room, you'll instantly be referred to a NEUROLOGIST for TESTS. If it happens to you at home while watching a Party Political Broadcast, this is perfectly normal.

NASAL HAIRS It's no good complaining of these – most Doctors have been trying to eradicate their own for several years. A quick peek up their nostrils while they're looking down your throat will confirm that they've failed dismally.

NASTY SWELLING OF THE ABDOMEN Excessive bloating of the stomach due to WIND, Faeces, Accumulated Fluid, Enlargement of an internal organ or a TUMOUR. Ladies should never rule out the possibility of PREGNANCY. If you notice a Nasty Swelling of the Abdomen, keep away from vets. They have a tendency to pierce the belly so excess air phsssssssts! away. Keep away from any Surgeon who might have spoken to a vet, too. These techniques have a tendency to propagate.

NATIONAL HEALTH SERVICE The mealy-mouthed bill-payers who do their damnedest to limit the number and quality of TESTS, DRUGS, consultations and OPERATIONS a Hypochondriac can have.

NAUSEOUS Inducing feelings of sickness. Take care not to say inadvertently to your Doctor 'I think I'm a bit nauseous'. He's all too likely to agree.

NEBULISER A device used to administer aerosoled drugs to the lungs through a face mask or mouth piece. Your Chest Physician is not taking you seriously as an Asthmatic unless he offers you one of these.

NEOPLASM Literally, new tissue. Like GROWTH this is a word frequently used in front of patients when a Doctor means CANCER, but doesn't want to say the word.

NEPHROLOGIST A Doctor specialising in the study of kidneys. Keep on friendly terms in case you ever need Dialysis, a Kidney Transplant, or spare organs for a Steak and Renal pie.

NERVE, TRAPPED Rather twee diagnosis for any IDI-OPATHIC Pain a doctor can't explain. Some cases are pukka – e.g., SCIATICA and CRUTCH PALSY. But if your twinge in the big toe, scrotum or left breast is ascribed merely to a Trapped Nerve, ask for a SECOND OPINION.

NEURALGIA# Doctor-impressing word for any Pain due to Irritation of a Nerve – e.g., Toothache. Some Neuralgias are difficult to treat – e.g., Trigeminal Neuralgia of the face and Post-Herpetic Neuralgia (after Shingles). Both of these warrant repeat trips to the Pain Clinic for the tender minis-trations of an Anaesthetist.

NEURAPRAXIA* A type of Nerve Injury in which the nerve looks OK from the outside, but internal damage or degeneration stops it passing electrical messages. Any twinge, weakness, pain or ache could be due to this – a useful diagnostic possibility to keep up your sleeve – and one that it is almost impossible for the Doctor to disprove.

NEURODERMATITIS An itchy, Eczema-like skin Rash due to repeated scratching. This is a much classier Disease to claim in place of ECZEMA or DERMATITIS. Upgrade immediately.

NEUROLOGIST A Doctor specialising in Diseases of the Nervous System. It's worth knowing that Neurologists and Psychiatrists hate each other's guts. You'll gain many brownie points by verbally sounding off about one in front of the other.

NEUROPSYCHIATRIST A PSYCHIATRIST who is bored playing with his allotted three Diseases and five drugs and is encroaching on the patch of the NEUROLOGIST. Neuropsychiatrists and Psychiatrists hate each other's guts even more than Neurologists and Psychiatrists do, so opportunities for even more brownie points.

NEUROMA A BENIGN TUMOUR of Nerve Tissue which, of course, in a Hypochondriac could always develop into a NEUROSARCOMA.

NEURONS# The Doctor-impressing word for Nerve Cells. We each possess billions that interconnect through branching DENDRITES and SYNAPSES (see diagram). There are three main types of Neurons: Interneurons, Motor Neurons and Sensory Neurons. The longest ones stretch from the spinal cord to the foot. You will gain credit with your Doctor if, when describing a tic, you say, 'I've got this Sub-occular Excitation of Motor Neurones.' When complaining of an

NEURONS

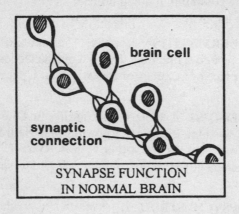

brain cell

synaptic connection

SYNAPSE FUNCTION
IN NORMAL BRAIN

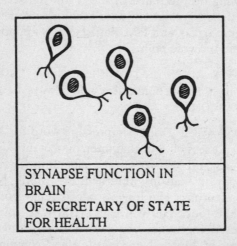

SYNAPSE FUNCTION IN
BRAIN
OF SECRETARY OF STATE
FOR HEALTH

itch, try saying, 'I've got a Tactile Problem with my Dermal Sensory Neurons.' That should send him rushing to the Medical Dictionary.

NEUROSARCOMA A medical term that describes a MALIGNANCY affecting a nerve.

NEUROSIS A Psychiatric disorder in which the sufferer is distressed, anxious, fearful, obsessive or mildly depressed whilst remaining in touch with reality. The only Neurosis most Hypochondriacs develop is an intense fear that perhaps, after all, there really is nothing wrong with them. That awful prospect would remove all meaning from their lives.

NEUROTRANSMITTER A chemical secreted by one NEURON to stimulate another. There are many different Transmitters, and too much or too little of them can cause Diseases such as Parkinson's, Alzheimer's, Schizophrenia, Bulimia and DEPRESSION. It's now quite trendy to claim a Neurotransmitter Problem. Use one as an excuse for a tantrum and a consultation with a NEUROLOGIST. But beware, you might get the NEUROPSYCHIATRIST instead.

'NIL BY MOUTH' A sign to strike terror in the heart of any Hypochondriac. How else are you going to tell people about your Symptoms?

NITRATES Drugs that dilate blood vessels and improve Blood Flow. These are used to treat complaints such as ANGINA PECTORIS and Heart Failure, but do have IATROGENIC SIDE EFFECTS. These include: Flushing, HEADACHE and possibly . . . an enormous ERECTION. Not many people complain of the latter, however.

NOCTURIA The infuriating Symptom of getting up at night to pass water. The only good thing about Nocturia is that, if your partner's also awake, you might be in with a chance of a bonk. Assuming you're up to it.

NODULE A small lump of tissue that protrudes from the skin surface – e.g., a POLYP, or is felt beneath – e.g., a GANGLION. Nodules are important, as they could be the first signs of CANCER. It's worth spending several hours a week surreptitiously examining your body for previously undiscovered Nodules, Lumps and LESIONS – but then of course all Hypochondriacs do that anyway.

NON-INVASIVE 1. A term used to describe any medical procedure that does not involve penetration of the skin or entry through an orifice. For example, an X-ray is Non-invasive, but a Digital Rectal Examination definitely isn't.
2. A term used to describe a form of questioning that neatly skips round the embarrassing bits. PSYCHIATRISTS are incapable of this delicate art. They're much too nosey.

NON-SPECIFIC URETHRITIS (NSU) Inflammation of the URETHRA due to anything other than Gonorrhoea. Sometimes also called Non-Gonococcal Urethritis. Symptoms include an embarrassing Discharge, stinging and burning on passing water. Sometimes, however, this condition is symptomless – so everyone can worry they've got it.

'NOT OUT OF THE WOODS YET' An expression much heard around hospitals, usually voiced by visitors who have just been to see a sick relative at VISITING TIME. It is used by Hypochondriacs in those agonising moments when the MEDICATION seems to be working and a CURE looks unavoidable. 'I'm not so sure,' you say with a gloomy shake of your head. 'I'm not out of the woods yet.'

NUMBNESS Loss of sensation in a part of the body due to

NOTIFIABLE DISEASE

A medical condition that must by law be reported to the Health Authority immediately. It's your Doctor's responsibility to do this, not yours, and he's paid something like 30p for the effort. But there's nothing to stop you phoning the Prime Minister and informing him you've got it, too. Notifiable diseases are something every **hypochondriac** should aim for. Tick them off on the following CHART as appropriate

Notifiable diseases   TICK WHEN SUSPECTED

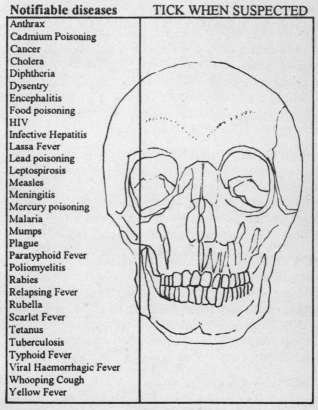

Anthrax
Cadmium Poisoning
Cancer
Cholera
Diphtheria
Dysentry
Encephalitis
Food poisoning
HIV
Infective Hepatitis
Lassa Fever
Lead poisoning
Leptospirosis
Measles
Meningitis
Mercury poisoning
Malaria
Mumps
Plague
Paratyphoid Fever
Poliomyelitis
Rabies
Relapsing Fever
Rubella
Scarlet Fever
Tetanus
Tuberculosis
Typhoid Fever
Viral Haemorrhagic Fever
Whooping Cough
Yellow Fever

the malfunctioning of Sensory NEURONS. Numbness is a desired IATROGENIC effect of Anaesthesia. Ensure that you insist on this for any procedure more painful than undressing for the examination.

NURSE A profession originally designed as a mere helpmate-cum-general-cleaner for terribly important hospital Doctors. Nurses have evolved at a great rate, however, and now have the power to tell a Doctor to sod off when he's upsetting one of their patients. Always get the Nurse on your side – then you can play her off against the Doctor.

O

OBSESSIVE-COMPULSIVE DISORDER A NEUROSIS which fills sufferers with obsessive thoughts and compels them to enact repeated, bizarre rituals. The commonest obsessions involve Cleanliness and Germs. Watch your Doctor carefully, and notice whether he washes his hands before and after every patient. If he does, it must mean he's a victim of an Obsessive-Compulsive Disorder, mustn't it?

OBSTETRICIAN A Doctor skilled in pulling a large object out of a much smaller hole. Most are also GYNAE-COLOGISTS and spend their day pot-holing round various female crevices.

OCCLUSION# Doctor-impressing word for Blockage in a passage, canal or blood vessel. If you want to impress your Doctor with the extent of your CONSTIPATION, try claiming an Occlusion of your rear MEATUS.

OCCULT A medical word meaning hidden or obscure. It commonly refers to an Occult Malignancy. Doctors invoke this word when they know you've got a Tumour but are buggered if they can find it. When you next get a HEAD-ACHE, try claiming an Occult, Space-occupying LESION – that should warrant a diagnostic Brain Scan and an appointment with a top NEUROLOGIST.

OCCULT BLOOD Hidden Blood, usually in the faeces. Doctors pick this up by smearing faeces on chemical paper and waiting for the colour to change. Kids get walloped for less.

OCCUPATIONAL DISEASE Any illness or injury resulting from one's work. Exposure to chemicals, dust, radiation or Infectious Disease fits this category. Good Occupational Diseases to complain of include: Back Pain; Stress; Skin Problems; Electric Shock; Lung Disease – e.g., Asthma; Deafness; VIBRATION WHITE FINGER; DERMATITIS; WORK-RELATED UPPER LIMB DISORDER (Repetitive Strain Injury by another name); and even some CANCERS. If you develop a recognised Occupational Disease, the financial benefits can be awesome. If you're an unemployed Hypochondriac – bad luck. This one's about as useful to you as a cut in the basic rate of Income Tax.

OESOPHAGITIS Inflammation of the gullet. This causes Heartburn due to acid regurgitating up from the stomach. You may have an Hiatus Hernia, which means TESTS, tests and more tests. If you want to impress your Doctor, rather than asking for another boring old Antacid, get him to prescribe you a PROKINETIC AGENT.

OESOPHAGOSCOPY Examination of the oesophagus by shoving down an Endoscope. This is usually the same one used for GASTROSCOPY. These days hospital ADMINISTRATORS quite often save money by insisting the Gastroenterologist uses a pen torch and lollipop stick instead.

OESTROGEN A group of female HORMONES that keep women curvaceous, juicy and young. This is prescribed as HRT once the ovaries retire at the MENOPAUSE. Men maintain that Oestrogen has a lot to answer for.

OLIGOSPERMIA The presence of only small numbers of sperm in the SEMEN. You may improve your sperm count by stopping smoking, laying off Alcohol and wearing cotton boxer shorts. Douche the TESTICLES in cold water (oooooh!)

at least once a day, and take supplements of Antioxidant Vitamins C, E and Betacarotene plus Mineral Zinc. These mop up damaging metabolic chemicals and prove that an orange a day helps the sperm on their way.

-OMA A suffix that implies a TUMOUR. These are usually BENIGN, but not always – e.g.:

Lipoma – a BENIGN Tumour of fat
Osteoma – a BENIGN Tumour of bone
Sarcoma – a MALIGNANT Tumour of bone, muscle or connective tissue
Carcinoma – a MALIGNANT Tumour in the surface layers or lining membrane of an organ
Oklahoma – a BENIGN musical.

ONCOLOGIST A Doctor who specialises in diagnosing and treating CANCER. The Hypochondriac's party trick is to imply that he needs the attentions of one, without actually doing so.

ONYCHOGRYPHOSIS# Doctor-impressing word for something very banal. If you go into the surgery and say 'I've got a touch of Onychogryphosis,' all it means is that your toe- or fingernails need clipping.

-OPATHY Suffix meaning Disease or disorder – e.g.:

Neuropathy – Disease of the nerves
Myopathy – Disease of the muscles
Psychopathy – Disease of the mind
Homeopathy – living in unhealthy conditions.

OPEN HEART SURGERY A Hypochondriac's most coveted operation – second only to a TRANSPLANT. The heart beat is temporarily stopped and your life placed in the hands of a cynical Heart-lung Bypass Machine. This is your chance of a Near-Death Experience – an event you can dine out on for many years to come.

OPERABLE A term describing any condition that can be treated through Surgical Intervention. For a Hypochondriac this can sometimes offer the daunting prospect of a complete CURE. But don't despair – even successful surgery can lead to POST-OPERATIVE COMPLICATIONS.

OPERATION Game in which one or more Surgeons enter your body and play Guess the Anatomy. Unfortunately, they often lose.

OPPORTUNISTIC SYMPTOM A problem to keep up your sleeve for when other Symptoms are dealt with too rapidly. These little gems can be easily introduced by phrases such as 'Oh, whilst I'm here, Doctor . . .' or 'Funny you should say that, I've got . . .'

ORAL CONTRACEPTIVES These are designed to prevent Pregnancy. This is achieved either by the female participant insisting on talking about the SIDE EFFECTS of Oral Contraceptives – or, even better, insisting on talking about 'our relationship'. Either way, the male participant will quickly lose interest in sex.

ORCHITIS Inflammation of one or both TESTICLES, often due to Mumps. Any Pain in the testicle should be investigated immediately. And you're advised to go to your doctor first, rather than consulting an Ophthalmologist about the tears the experience brought to your eyes.

ORGANIC 1. A problem is said to be Organic when it is physiological rather than psychological.
2. A person is said to be Organic when they are totally

illogical about conflicting environmental data they have read in the *Guardian*.

ORGAN DONATION Make sure you've definitely finished with your Organ before offering it for Donation as mistakes can rarely be rectified afterwards.

ORIENTAL SORE Also known as the Baghdad Boil, this is an Infection transmitted by sandflies. Starting as an itchy Papule, the Sore enlarges over a period of weeks and becomes ulcerated. Hypochondriacs are advised against complaining of this to their Doctors as the lack of sandflies in this country may be a bit of a giveaway.

ORTHOPNOEA Difficulty in breathing when lying flat, usually due to excess fluid on the lungs. Doctors assess the severity of this Symptom by asking how many pillows you use at night. Always say four – the fact that you throw all but one to the floor should not come between you and a possible REFERRAL or Diagnostic Investigation.

OSTEOMALACIA Literally, Bad Bones. Softening, Weakness and Demineralisation are due to lack of Vitamin D. This is essential for absorbing Calcium and Phosphorus from the diet. The best way to get Vitamin D is exposure to sunlight – so demand a trip to the Caribbean at NHS expense.

OSTEOPATHY A complementary system of Diagnosis and treatment based on the Musculoskeletal System. Beware – you may well have met your match, as Osteopaths are prime manipulators too.

OTORRHOEA# Doctor-impressing word for a discharge from the ear.

OTOSCLEROSIS A common, inherited cause of Deafness.

A tiny bone in the middle ear overgrows and stops sound vibrations passing to the inner ear. Request a Hearing Test, and hold out for a Stapedectomy. This OPERATION replaces the culprit with an artificial bone, thus producing a CURE. But don't worry – there's nothing to stop you continuing to pretend that you're still deaf.

OTOTOXICITY Toxic damage to the inner ear due to certain drugs. When feeling bored, it's always worth asking if any of your drugs are Ototoxic.

'OUT-OF-BODY EXPERIENCE' Something with which the seasoned Hypochondriac, who has actually been at DEATH'S DOOR, can bore everyone for years.

OUTPATIENT TREATMENT Poor substitute for the real thing – which is of course In-patient Care. Most Hypochondriacs, though – as they find out to their cost – receive impatient care.

P

PAEDIATRICIAN A Doctor who specialises in childish behaviour. Go easy on him, he really can't help it.

PAINKILLERS Drugs that relieve discomfort so you can concentrate on describing your Symptoms. It's worth not taking them every now and then to remind yourself how bad your Pain really is.

PALPATION A medical word which makes it all right for a Doctor to feel you up.

PALPITATION Rapid beating of your heart whilst the Doctor is performing a PALPATION.

PASSING WATER Colloquial expression for MICTURITION or urination. Hypochondriacs who have difficulties in Passing Water are advised always to take their swimming things with them.

PATHOGNOMONIC A word that means a Symptom or sign is diagnostic of a particular condition – e.g., KOPLIK'S SPOTS are diagnostic of MEASLES; lipstick on the collar is diagnostic of an extra-marital affair, etc.

PELVIC INFLAMMATORY DISEASE (PID) An Infection of the Internal Female Sexual Organs. If you are male and are told you have PID, don't panic – you haven't had an OCCULT sexual reassignment. The initials PID are also used to mean Prolapsed Intervertebral Disc.

PENILE IMPLANT Penile Implants may be inserted to

PAIN

A **hypochondriac's** oldest and dearest friend.
Doctors place much store by the way patients describe
their Pain. Have a look at the CHART below and
choose the most apt descriptions.

Pain Descriptions
Aching
Gnawing
Dragging
Throbbing
Stabbing
Burning
Stinging
Sharp
Dull
Crushing
Tight
Constant
Comes and goes in waves
Colicky
Deep
Superficial
Sort of tingly
Like someone dribbling melted ice down my back
As if someone's pushed a stick of celery into me and is turning it
round
All sort of flubbery and woofly

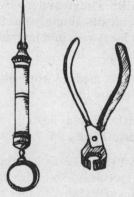

Worse or better on breathing in
Worse or better on leaning forward
Worse, better or triggered by eating
Radiates [Spreads] to elsewhere on the body
Continuous Agony [the **hypochondriac's** favourite]

Then decide on how bad your pain is, on a scale of 1—10
where: 1 is a little twinge
10 is the worst pain you could ever imagine

104

increase the cosmetic thickness of the male organ, or to allow men previously suffering from IMPOTENCE to sustain an ERECTION. Implants often possess a start button which you should be careful not to activate in the wrong place – e.g., the checkout at Tesco.

PENIS The male sex organ which, through some divine oversight, manages to transmit both urine and SEMEN. Luckily, an inflatable bung prevents the one happening simultaneously with the other. The trick is to know which you want and to go for it before the bung changes its mind.

PENIS, CANCER OF THE Every male Hypochondriac's ultimate nightmare. Use this as an excuse to finger – sorry, examine – yours as often as you like. See MASTURBATION, EXCESSIVE.

PENIS SIZE See diagram on page 106.

PERFORATION A hole made in any part of the body due to Disease or Injury. The commonest Perforations are of the tympanic membrane in the ear, and a Perforated Peptic Ulcer. Some people pick their nose so vigorously that they excavate a hole right through the nasal septum dividing the nostrils. If you do this, say the damage was caused by sniffing cocaine – it sounds better.

PERVERSIONS, DANGEROUS Unwise practices involving foreplay, forearms, four-ply and firearms – not necessarily in that order. Best avoided unless you're trying to frighten your PSYCHIATRIST by telling him about them. Anyway, forget it – Psychiatrists can absorb and better anything their patients are likely to dream up.

PETROLEUM JELLY An ointment base that can be used to facilitate sexual congress. For example, it can be smeared on

ERECT PENIS SIZE [HUMAN MALE]

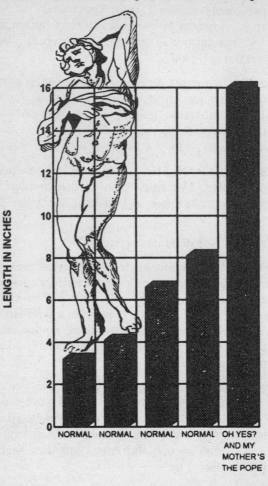

the doorknob to prevent kids entering their parents' bedroom unexpectedly.

PHANTOM LIMB The perception that a limb is still present after amputation. Amputees often complain of Pain in their Phantom Limbs – which comes as no surprise to Hypochondriacs, who are used to feeling Pain that no one else believes in.

PHIMOSIS Tightness of the foreskin such that it can't be pulled back over the head of the PENIS. This is normal during the first year of life, and the foreskin should never be forcibly retracted. Older males may need an operation to prevent an accidental self-circumcision whilst making love.

PHOBIA Baseless and irrational fear. This condition is never experienced by Hypochondriacs, who always know that their fears are absolutely real.

PIGEON-HOLED The tendency for patients, especially Hypochondriacs, to be permanently labelled – usually with unflattering descriptions – e.g., Neurotic, OBSESSIVE-COMPULSIVE, TATSP or worst of the lot – HYPOCHONDRIAC.

PILES One of those ailments that is terribly funny to everyone except the sufferer.

PINGUECULA A small, yellowish spot on the white of the eye. From the medical point of view, this is nothing to worry about, but don't let that stop you.

PLACEBO An inactive substance given to a patient who is led to believe it's a wonder drug to cure their problems. Doctors have a nasty habit of prescribing these to Hypochondriacs, so you should always ask suspiciously 'Is this a Placebo?' whenever a too-good-to-be-true drug is prescribed. And a really sophisticated Hypochondriac will ensure that even a Placebo produces SIDE EFFECTS.

PLACEBO EFFECT The miraculous improvement or CURE due to a patient's faith and expectations of a prescribed substance – even though it is chemically inactive. A dirty trick for a Doctor to play on any Hypochondriac.

PLASTER CAST A protective Plaster of Paris splint that is moulded round a limb and allowed to harden. Hypochondriacs should be ambivalent about these. Though your being put in Plaster is a testament to the fact that there really is something wrong with you, no true Hypochondriac wishes ever to be dismissed as merely accident-prone.

PLASTIC SURGERY 1. Reconstructive surgery performed on skin damaged by injury or Disease.
2. Cosmetic surgery performed on skin damaged by the ravages of time and too much eating.
3. Yet another example of cost-cutting in the NHS. In the old days surgeries used to be built of bricks and mortar.

PLICATION A type of Surgical Tuck that is stitched in place to decrease an organ's size. A Tuck in the diaphragm can treat Hiatus Hernia, a Tuck in the stomach can treat obesity. Any man who says he's had a Plication of the Penis is:

A) showing off, and
B) lying.

PNEUMONIA Inflammation or Infection of the lungs. Double Pneumonia is twice as bad – both lungs are affected. You are advised against claiming Triple Pneumonia – even the average GP knows enough anatomy to catch you out on that one.

POLYDIPSIA Excessive Thirst, which is a common Symptom of DIABETES, Dehydration and HANGOVER. Introducing more fluid into the system is the recommended treatment for all three conditions – but particularly Hangover.

POLYSYMPTOMATIC Describes the existence of many Symptoms usually at the same time. In classic HYPOCHONDRIASIS, these flit round the body – as soon as one is dealt with, make sure you have another one ready to take its place.

PORPHYRIA A group of rare inherited Metabolic Disorders in which chemicals formed during the manufacture of Haemoglobin – the Porphyrins – build up in the blood. One form, Congenital Erythropoietic Porphyria, causes:

> Blistering when skin is exposed to sunlight, so sufferers only come out at night
> Red Discolouration of the eyes and teeth
> Red Discolouration of stale urine
> Excessive Hairiness
> Anaemia and Paleness from lack of Iron.

This Disease is the basis of the vampire myth. Claim it at your peril. If your Symptoms are too convincing, the Doctor might end up putting a stake through your heart.

POSITIVE The coveted yet feared result of any TEST. This means a DIAGNOSIS is close at hand.

POST MORTEM The Hypochondriac's final accolade. Having achieved the life-time's ambition of proving he or she really was ill, the Hypochondriac will have ensured that the Death was from something sufficiently puzzling to justify further investigation.

POST-OPERATIVE COMPLICATIONS Problems that develop after an operation – e.g., PNEUMONIA due to the Anaesthetic; a skin Infection from the Fluid Drip; Cystitis from the CATHETERISATION; Paralytic Ileus from the manhandling of your bowels; a Giant Crush on the dishy Surgeon who did the handling.

PRACTICE The seat of operations for a General Practitioner. The word does not inspire confidence, suggesting that the Doctor may regard his patients as more disposable than they might wish.

PRE-CANCEROUS A change in a previously BENIGN condition that renders it likely to turn MALIGNANT. All Hypochondriac conditions are Pre-Cancerous.

PREGNANCY A Menstrual Cycle lasting approximately forty-six weeks from the start of the last period until the beginning of the next. For some reason, around six weeks before the end of this prolonged Cycle, a baby pops out. The good thing about Pregnancy is that it brings a whole pile of new problems to worry about: INDIGESTION, Heartburn, VARICOSE VEINS, PILES – to name just a few.

PREGNANCY, FALSE The delusion of Pregnancy in which real physical signs develop – e.g., MORNING SICKNESS, Breast Enlargement, Abdominal Swelling, despite Pregnancy Tests remaining Negative. Doctors call this Pseudocyesis, and don't know why it occurs. Perhaps it's an advanced case of Hypochondriasis, where all the Symptoms of Pregnancy can be enjoyed without the little sod at the end.

PREMATURE EJACULATION The ultimate in getting ahead with the job.

PREMENSTRUAL SYNDROME (PMS) A collection of Symptoms occurring between Ovulation and Menstruation. Female Hypochondriacs have to take care that their Symptoms aren't all blamed on this. If you're told your problems are due to PMS, try stating firmly that you have 'Menstrual

Magnification of a Pre-existing Disorder'. That should flummox the average GP.

PRE-OPERATIVE COMPLICATIONS Problems occurring just before your operation. These include:

Being booked in for the wrong operation
Having the wrong limb marked for amputation
Falling off the operating table and breaking a leg
Falling in love with the Anaesthetist (when did you last meet someone who made you go so woozy and weak at the knees?).

PREPUCE Bit of the male anatomy that sounds like it might turn garish purple whilst limbering up for action – as indeed it frequently does. Also known as the foreskin.

PRESBYOPIA Progressive loss of near vision with increasing age. This is due to a loss of Accommodation. Once you've found somewhere else to stay, ask your Doctor for a REFERRAL to an Opthalmologist.

PRESCRIPTION That without which no self-respecting Hypochondriac will leave the Doctor's surgery.

PRESCRIPTION CHARGE Money paid to free your necessary MEDICATION from ransom. As Hypochondriacs need more drugs than the average Doctor-user, it seems unfair that you should shoulder the cost. If you are one of the few who actually pay the Prescription Charge, see if you have any of the following Symptoms, which will qualify you for exemption:

Underactive Thyroid Gland.
Underactive Parathyroid Glands
Underactive Pituitary Glands
Underactive Adrenal Glands

111

Underactive Pancreas, causing DIABETES MELLITUS (unless controlled by diet alone)

Permanent Fistula

A Muscle Disease called Myasthenia Gravis

Epilepsy requiring Continuous Therapy

Any physical disability that permanently prevents you leaving your normal residence without someone to help you

Pregnancy and the year after delivery.

Hypochondriasis where the story is convincing enough for a Doctor to verify one of the above.

PROCTALGIA FUGAX An elegant-sounding name for a rather inelegant complaint – a severe cramp-like Pain in the rectum. It is not in fact related to any Disease, but is usually due to Muscle Spasm, occasionally from STRESS or ANXIETY. Still, it's a useful expression when you want to vent your feelings of annoyance about someone (non-medical). Just call them a 'Proctalgia Fugax'. They won't know what you mean – but you will!

PROCTOLOGIST A bit of a bum job, really.

PROKINETIC AGENT State-of-the-art anti-reflux drug which cures Indigestion by forcing stomach secretions downwards and stopping them flowing up. As many Doctors prescribe cheap Antacids for Heartburn, try requesting a Prokinetic Agent instead.

PROSTATE The Prostate Gland is the size and shape of a large chestnut (though you're not advised to try playing conkers with it). It's situated between the bladder and PENIS, wrapped round the URETHRA. After the age of about forty it naturally starts to enlarge. This is the ultimate time-bomb ticking deep in the plumbing of every male.

PSYCHIATRIST A specialist with a declared interest in studying, preventing and treating Mental Illness, Emotional or Behavioural Problems. They seem to do this by demonstrating most of the Symptoms themselves – presumably with a view to putting their patients at ease.

PSYCHOSOMATIC The perception of physical Symptoms that are caused by, or worsened by, psychological problems such as Emotional Stress. Conditions such as HEADACHE, Shortness of Breath, IRRITABLE BOWEL SYNDROME and ECZEMA have all acquired Psychosomatic labels in the past. Hypochondriacs have nothing to do with this word. When they're ill, they're *really* ill.

PUDENDA# A Doctor-impressing word for the female, external naughty bits.

PULMONARY EMBOLISM Literally, a wandering Clot that lodges in the lung. These often break off from a THROMBUS in the deep veins of the leg, and can be LIFE-THREATENING. Twice as many women as men are affected, as Pregnancy and being on the Contraceptive Pill add to other risks such as IMMOBILITY and recent surgery. So female Hypochondriacs are justified in being doubly anxious about this condition.

PULSE The rhythmic, wave-like Dilation and Contraction of an artery as blood is pumped round the body by the heart. Pulses are most easily felt in the neck (Carotid), wrist (Radial) and at the top of the leg (Femoral). A Hypochondriac will feel for all of these pulses at least once an hour – and quite frequently have a Panic Attack when he can't find them.

PUS Yuk.

Q

QUARANTINE The isolation of a person or animal recently exposed to a CONTAGIOUS INFECTION. Isolation is usually for longer than the suspected INCUBATION PERIOD. Try not to get quarantined against Infection with a Slow Virus Disease – you could be out of circulation for several decades.

QUICKENING The moment when an expectant mother first becomes aware of something moving around in her stomach. See also TAPEWORM; FLATULENCE; ALIEN.

QUINSY An ABSCESS on a tonsil. This causes a severe SORE THROAT, FEVER and difficulty in swallowing due to the massive one-sided (occasionally bilateral) swelling. The fauces become swollen and discoloured. No, stop all that anxious peering down the loo: *Fauces* – meaning the narrow opening between the mouth and the throat.

R

RABIES A viral Infection of the Nervous System, transmitted by the bite of an infected animal. The INCUBATION PERIOD is anywhere from nine days to many months, so if you've been bitten by anything larger than a flea (e.g., a drunken lover) during the last year, there's still time for worrying. The opening of the Channel Tunnel provides further cause for concern.

RADIOLOGY A branch of medicine that investigates, diagnoses and treats Disease by passing Radioactive (and other remarkably complicated substances) through your body. If the Disease doesn't get you, the Radiology might. Always cover your gonads with a lead shield to preserve the family heirlooms.

RADIONUCLIDE SCAN State-of-the-art Radiological Investigation, which any self-respecting Hypochondriac should aim to experience at least once.

RASH 1. A selection of spots, LESIONS and Erythema (reddening) on the skin. These are usually temporary, unless brought on by a Psychotic tattooist. If your rash is accompanied by FEVER and ITCHING, congratulations – you have probably contracted some dreadful Disease.
2. Too-rapid decision on your part that Symptoms are not due to a nasty, Malignant, Contagious or otherwise LIFE-THREATENING Disease. In future, use your imagination more fruitfully.

RECOVERY, COMPLETE A condition which no Hypochondriac will either experience or contemplate.

RECOVERY POSITION The correct position in which to place someone who is unconscious. This could well be propped up against the bar with a drink close to their right arm and a strategically placed bucket by their left.

RECTALGIA# Doctor-impressing word – and insulting word to describe non-doctors – for a Pain in the Arse. See PROCTALGIA FUGAX.

RECTAL THERMOMETER An instrument designed to take the body temperature via the rectum. A Consultant recently tried signing a cheque with one of these before exclaiming 'Some bum's got my biro'.

RECTUM Well, it certainly didn't do 'em any good.

REFERRAL One of the Hypochondriac's ultimate aims. Any visit to the Doctor's surgery that ends in Referral to a CONSULTANT is a justified triumph.

REFERRED PAIN* 1. A Pain felt in a part of the body that is distant from the site of its cause – e.g., heart Pain is often felt in the arm; APPENDICITIS starts off round the umbilicus (belly button). The perfect solution for all Hypochondriacs, who are thus enabled to attribute discomfort felt anywhere in their body to a LIFE-THREATENING Disease sited anywhere else in their body.
2. Hypochondriac shunted off to the GP trainee.

REGRESSION The psychoanalytical return to childhood when under STRESS. If you find yourself sleeping in a foetal position, sucking your thumb or fondling your genitalia, you may well have regressed – or you may just be enjoying yourself.

RELAPSE A wonderful occasion when a favourite Symptom you thought you'd lost forever pays a return visit. Rush off to tell the doctor straight away.

REMISSION An upsetting concept. Life without Symptoms is unbearable. Resort to an OPPORTUNISTIC SYMPTOM.

REPETITIVE STRAIN INJURY (RSI) Don't use this phrase any more – a doddery old judge may tell you the condition doesn't exist. Go for WORK-RELATED UPPER LIMB DISORDER and plenty of compensation.

RESPIRATORY ARREST# Doctor-impressing phrase meaning No Longer Breathing. The trouble is, if you've got it, you won't have the opportunity to impress the doctor with it.

RESTLESS LEGS SYNDROME An unpleasant, insistent need to move one's legs – frequently occurring just before dozing off. More common in smokers, those who drinks lots of caffeine, and in PREGNANCY. If you suffer from it, you will impress your Doctor more by calling it von Ekbom's Disease.

REVERSE VASECTOMY Ymotcesav.

REVOLVING DOOR SYNDROME A classic case of a patient being discharged too soon from a Psychiatric Hospital and bouncing straight back in again – a cycle that tends to go round and round and on and on. Also common with Hypochondriacs, who manage to develop new Symptoms before getting out of the surgery door.

RHEUMATOID ARTHRITIS Serious Inflammatory Disease of the joints, in which your IMMUNE SYSTEM cocks it up by making self-attacking Antibodies. As one standard treatment is with regular Gold Injections, you may soon be worth a fortune.

RHINITIS# Doctor-impressing word for a Red Nose. You might try to impress your Doctor even more by saying you're suffering from RUDOLPH'S SYNDROME, but there's always a danger he'll work it out.

RHINOPHYMA A bulbous, red deformity of the end of the nose. This usually occurs in elderly males as a COMPLICATION of ROSACEA. Not to be confused with COMIC RELIEF.

RHINOPLASTY Doctor-impressing word for Nose Job.

RIB The spare bit that Adam donated for the benefit of all mankind. Many women wish he'd given up another spare bit instead.

RIGOR MORTIS Something which reinforces the fact that a Hypochondriac was right all along.

RINGWORM A Fungal skin Infection that forms scaly ring-shaped patches on the skin. Diagnosis can be aided by the use of ultra-violet light under which areas of Fungal Infection show up fluorescent. So if you think you might have Ringworm, choose your disco with care!

RORSCHACH TEST Psychoanalytical technique in which you're shown an ink blot and asked what it makes you think of. See diagram for typical Hypochondriac Rorschach Test result.

ROSACEA A CHRONIC skin condition in which the nose and cheeks look permanently red. Flushing is worse after Alcohol or spicy food and sometimes, Pustules erupt. Inexperienced Doctors have been known to diagnose Rosacea in

RORSCHACH TEST
....Typical **Hypochondriac's** Result

INK BLOT
What it made the patient think of

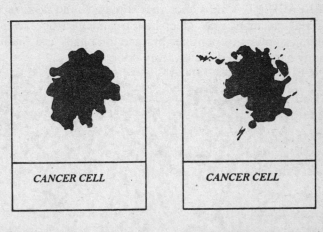

CANCER CELL	*CANCER CELL*

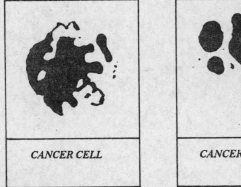 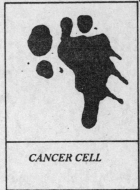

CANCER CELL	*CANCER CELL*

patients who've come to see them about PILES, IMPOTENCE or embarrassing BORBORYGMI.

ROUGHAGE 1. Fibre in the diet that keeps the bowels regular, discouraging CONSTIPATION and IRRITABLE BOWEL SYNDROME.
2. Approximate estimation of how old someone is.

RUBEFACIENT A substance that stimulates the skin, turning it red and acting like a deep heat treatment. Rubefacients include camphor, turpentine, pan scouring pads and finding Granny hasn't locked the lavatory door.

S

SADDLEBAG SCROTUM SYNDROME A condition where the scrotum overhangs the PENIS like a shawl. There is no foundation to the rumours that John Wayne was a sufferer from this.

SADS* Seasonal Affective Disorder Syndrome is a form of DEPRESSION only occurring in the winter months and believed to be caused by sunlight deprivation. This is an excellent complaint for Hypochondriacs because, as with all forms of Depression, the Doctor's only got your word for how you're feeling. It's also an ideal excuse for that spare tyre mysteriously discovered in the spring. Demand Phototherapy – or a trip to the Seychelles – on the NHS.

SAFE PERIOD Time of the month when you thought you couldn't get Pregnant. This method of Contraception is not to be relied on – or you wouldn't be reading this book now.

SAFE SEX A statistical impossibility.

SAFER SEX Sexual activity occurring:

A) During the SAFE PERIOD
B) With Condoms or Dental Dams
C) With oneself. (This is probably the safest – if you can stand the company.)

SATURATED FATS 1. Delicious additions to the DIET that are currently saturating the health press. These are easily recognised, as they are all fattening, sinful, naughty but nice.
2. Rejected *Sun* headline on the day of Robert Maxwell's death.

SCAPHOID* This is a Hypochondriac's (and a lawyer's) dream, because it is the most litigious bone in the body. Just say your wrist hurts; that you once broke your Scaphoid and the Diagnosis was appallingly manhandled. Before you've drawn breath – let alone your first SICK NOTE – you'll be in PLASTER from your thumb to your elbow for six weeks, and in with a good chance of being awarded damages.

SCARRED FOR LIFE The Hypochondriac's ultimate accolade.

SCIATICA* Neuralgic Pain related to the sciatic nerve, and a gift Symptom to all Hypochondriacs. Since nothing shows on the outside, and since with a little practice anyone can master the authentically agonised Gait that goes with the condition, complaints of Sciatica can really flummox your Doctor. A useful accompanying phrase is 'Doctor, it only hurts when I————.' (Fill in the activity that you're trying to get out of.)

SECOND OPINION Something that Hypochondriacs insist on in all circumstances – unless of course the First Opinion is that your Symptoms are genuine.

SECONDARIES Affliction arising as a result of some other (Primary) affliction. Most often used when discussing CANCER but you shouldn't let that inhibit you. The really dedicated Hypochondriac can get Secondaries with a hangnail.

SECRECY, MEDICAL Now that everyone has the right to read their own Medical Notes, Physicians resort to private shorthand to express their secret opinions of their patients. Abbreviations the curious Hypochondriac should watch out for include:

ABS – Absent Brain Syndrome
GOK – God Only Knows (what's wrong with this patient)
DFTNA – Dead From The Neck Up
NAGB – Needs A Good Bonk.

SECRETIONS These are usually pretty nasty. Most Doctors respond to the line 'I've got this Secretion' by yelling 'Nurse!' Brown Secretions are more unpleasant than yellow/green ones on the hole (*sic*).

SELENIUM DEFICIENCY Selenium is a trace element, and another gift to the Hypochondriac. Selenium Deficiency is linked with a multitude of Symptoms that so far have not been substantiated. Most Doctors have heard of Selenium, but can't remember why. Therefore, if you tell them you've been diagnosed as having———— (fill in the Symptom of your choice) as a result of Selenium Deficiency, they will tend to believe you.

SEMEN Politically incorrect term now rejected by radical feminists in favour of Sewomen.

SEPTICAEMIA Blood Poisoning. The first thing a Hypochondriac thinks of when pricking his or her finger with a needle.

SHOCK Trauma suffered by patient in hospital on discovering how much *isn't* included in the Private Healthcare Plan to which contributions have been made over many years.

SHORTNESS Do not go to your Doctor complaining of this. There is very little he can do about it. Besides, he probably won't be able to see you over the desk.

SICK NOTE One of the Hypochondriac's ultimate ambitions.

SICK SINUS SYNDROME If your Doctor says you've got this and your nose isn't stuffed up, it's serious, because the sinus involved is the electrical node which keeps your heart beating at a regular pace. Demand a Pacemaker, and when he drops out of the race, ask for an electric one.

SIDE EFFECTS* Something all Hypochondriacs rely on. Just when the Doctor's diagnosed your Disease, prescribed a medication to cure it, and reckons that should keep you out of his surgery for a few weeks, then it's the moment to . . . bring on the Side Effects!

'SIZE DOESN'T MATTER' A delusion fostered by:

A) Agony aunts
B) Altruistic women
C) Underendowed men.

SMALLPOX 1. Sexual Infection in C) above.
2. A Disease related to Chickenpox but a million times worse. Sadly, you can't claim to have this nowadays. Smallpox is extinct except in two test-tubes – one in Portland Down and the other in . . . well, hopefully not Baghdad.

SORE THROAT This is guaranteed to get you in and out of your Doctor's surgery in two seconds flat. You're wasting your time with this if you want to be taken seriously. No self-respecting Hypochondriac would even bother with it.

SPECIMEN An interesting phenomenon always occurs when patients are asked to provide a Specimen. Delivery of it suddenly assumes all the difficulty of earning a Nobel Prize in Astrophysics. Specimens you are most likely to be asked for

SPERMATAZOA

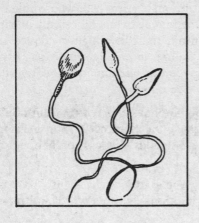

IT IS QUITE
SAFE TO GET
IMPREGNATED
BY THESE.

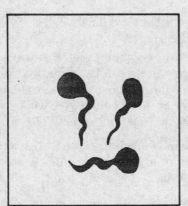

TRY TO AVOID
GETTING
IMPREGNATED
BY THESE. THE
CHANCE OF
GIVING BIRTH
TO A PRINCE
ARE MINIMAL.

– and try not to get them mixed up – include:

A) Mid-stream Urine (MSU)
B) Semen or Post-coital Cervical Mucus
C) Your signature on the Doctor's claim form.

SPERMATOZOA The mature male germ-cell, whose role in life is the impregnation of the female ovum. Since only one in millions achieve this ambition, there is a high incidence of DEPRESSION and sense of failure among Spermatozoa. Psychologists have so far not given this phenomenon the investigation it perhaps deserves. See diagram.

SPERMATOZOON The single of SPERMATOZOA. But don't bother with this word, because the chances of your meeting one on its own are extremely slender – unless you happen to be an ovum.

STIRRUPS For female Hypochondriacs the sight of these stimulates immediate Lacrimation – in other words, it brings tears to your eyes.

STITCHES The Hypochondriac's campaign medals. See diagram for varieties of Stitching available.

STRESS A feeling that the world is getting on top of you and that you can no longer cope. Stress can be caused by work pressures, domestic pressures or anything you wish to name, really. For classic Symptoms of the condition, see what your Doctor looks like just after you've left his surgery.

SUPERINFECTION A second Infection caused by a separate germ during the course of an initial Infection. As such, highly prized by Hypochondriacs – hence the name.

SWAB A word recurring with great frequency in any television scene set in an operating theatre.

VARIETY OF STITCHES

SUBCUTICULAR	————————————
INTERRUPTED	┼┼┼┼┼┼┼┼┼┼
CONTINUOUS	∿∿∿∿∿
INEPT	⌇⌇⌇⌇⌇
SURGEON SHOWING OFF	

SYMPTOMS These are the essential stock-in-trade of the dedicated Hypochondriac. There is no point in going to your Doctor without an adequate supply of Symptoms, and the best ones are those which might be trivial but could be indicators of some authentically serious disorder. For the Hypochondriac's convenience, examples of these good ambiguous ones are marked throughout the book with an asterisk (*).

SYNAPSE Also known as a Neuronal Junction, this is the functional connection between two nerve cells, which allows nerve impulses and information to be transmitted from one cell to the next. The Synapse directs the conduction of nerve impulses in regular circuits, preventing random stimulation of nerves and waste of energy.

SYNDROME If you're diagnosed as suffering from a DIS-EASE, bad luck. Your Symptoms date from the nineteenth century or before. Try changing them. Syndromes date from the twentieth century and are much classier.

They are also a gift to Hypochondriacs. Since new Syndromes are described almost daily, all you have to do is choose your Symptoms, select a name for your Syndrome and most Doctors will be none the wiser.

Or if you prefer, just present the Symptoms and leave it to your Doctor to do the labelling. If in this way you find yourself the proud owner of a Syndrome, congratulations! You are suffering from a problem that is state-of-the-art and testing the frontiers of medical science. Alternatively, your Doctor is totally foxed.

T

TATT 'Tired All The Time'. See JUNIOR DOCTORS.

TACHYCARDIA# Doctor-impressing word for Rapid Heartbeat.

TALOIA If your Doctor says you are suffering from this, do not be fooled. It simply stands for 'There's A Lot Of It About'.

TASTE Using expressions like Passing Water, Bowel Movement or Flatus rather than the alternatives.

TASTE, LACK OF 1. An unusual medical condition known as Ageusia – the Taste equivalent of Blindness or Deafness. 2. A more common medical condition, Symptoms of which include the purchase of this book.

TELANGIECTASIA# Doctor-impressing word for those 'broken' thread veins on your cheek and – if you've really been overdoing it – on your nose as well.

TEMPERATURE Something every good Hypochondriac should take at least once per day – ideally just after drinking a mug of hot tea.

TENDER OESOPHAGUS SYNDROME Frequently associated with Vindaloo curries and cheap plonk.

TENNIS ELBOW 1. Inflammation of the tendon attaching forearm muscles to the elbow. It can be due to playing tennis with a faulty grip, or any repetitive motion such as using a screwdriver or flicking through the pages of *The Hypochondriac's Dictionary of Ill Health*.

2. Something received by British players in the first round of Grand Slam tournaments.

TENOSYNOVITIS Not the name of a Russian dissident – though it should be – but in fact an Inflammation of the thin synovial MEMBRANE lining the sheath that surrounds a tendon.

TENOVAGINITIS Inflammation of the thick, fibrous wall of a sheath surrounding a tendon. If, when a female Hypochondriac complains of this, the Doctor asks her to undress and gets his Stirrups out, then he probably misheard what she said.

TERMINAL ILLNESS Though it sounds like a morbid fear of airports (*cf.* Sick Building Syndrome), this is in fact the ultimate aim of the truly dedicated Hypochondriac.

TESTICLES Not in fact a Greek philosopher, but the male reproductive glands, which are suspended by spermatic cords in the scrotum. The word originally meant 'small TESTIS', but now the two expressions are used interchangeably, possible proof of the theory that 'size isn't everything'.

TESTES Plural of TESTIS. Balls.

TESTIS Singular of TESTES. Ball.

TEST MATCH Ball Game.

TEST MATCH AGAINST THE WEST INDIES Whole different Ball Game.

TESTOSTERONE The male Sex Hormone that puts hairs on your chest, a beard on your face, muscles on your muscles and generally has a lot to answer for.

THEATRE Properly Operating Theatre, the room in which

TESTS

Investigations that shed light on symptoms and elucidate a DIAGNOSIS [q.v.]. A **hypochondriac's** life revolves around Medical Tests and their results. Try to aim for a minimum of 10 in any one year. Tick them off on the CHART below as you survive them:

Test	Date Performed	Result
Full Blood Count		
Urea & electrolytes		
Liver Function Tests		
Thyroid Function Tests		
Cardiac Enzymes		
Specific Hormone Levels		
Blood Clotting Time		
Platelet Count		
Blood Viscosity		
Auto Antibody Screen		
Blood Type		
Viral Antibody Screen		
HIV		
Syphilis		
X-ray		
CAT Scan		
MRI Scan		
PET Scan		
Radio Nuclide Scan		
Ultrasound		
Mammogram		
Pregnancy Test		
Chromosome Analysis		
Semen Analysis		
Cervical Smear		
Urogram		
Faecal Occult Blood		
Lumbar Puncture		
Liver Biopsy		
Kidney Biopsy		
Jejunal Test		

Continued:-

Angiogram		
Cholangiogram		
Cholecystogram		
Lymphangiogram		
Venogram		
Myelogram		
ECG		
EEG		
Echocardiogram		
Peak Flow		
Spirometry		
Endoscopy		
Gastroscopy		
Oesophagoscopy		
Colonoscopy		
Sigmoidoscopy		
Proctoscopy		
Laparoscopy		
Cystoscopy		
Bronchoscopy		
Swab for infectious organisms		
Intelligence Test		
Breathalyser [why not?]		
+Lie Detector Test		

+ Hypochondriacs are advised to be very cautious about taking this one.

OPERATIONS are conducted. If you want to know why it's called a Theatre, just watch some of the hammy performances Surgeons give therein. See GASTROSCOPY.

THICK NOTES SYNDROME Another sign of a successful and dedicated Hypochondriac. Your Doctor will already have TENNIS ELBOW from flicking through your specialists' letters and copious consultation notes.

THROMBUS A blood clot. Useful insult to hurl at someone you don't like. 'You great Thrombus!' is less likely to cause EPISTAXIS than 'You great dickhead!'

THRUSH A Fungal Infection causing a speckled Rash on a mucus MEMBRANE, for example in the VAGINA, that to some twit in the past resembled the markings on a thrush breast. Makes one wonder where he did his birdwatching.

THYROTOXICOSIS The Toxic Effects of an Overactive Thyroid Gland. These include:

Fast Metabolic Rate
Increased Appetite
Weight Loss
Feeling the Heat
Sweating
Flushed Skin
Racing Pulse
PALPITATIONS
Tremor
ANXIETY
Irritability
Bulging Eyes
Difficulty Sleeping

Heart Murmurs
Psychosis
Racing Thoughts (e.g., What won the 3.30 at
    Kempton?).

In other words, it offers a field day to the enthusiastic Hypochondriac. The only good thing about Thyrotoxicosis for non-Hypochondriacs is that it makes you burn up Alcohol faster than normal, so you are less likely to fail a Breathalyser Test.

TINNITUS Bizarre and disturbing ringing, buzzing, whistling or hissing noises heard in the ear. Before going to the Doctor complaining of this, take that Two Unlimited cassette out of your Walkman.

TINTINUS The tendency of intrepid boy reporters' hair to go up in an unlikely quiff at the front.

TOLERANCE 1. The need to take an increasingly large dose of a drug – e.g., Alcohol, Morphine or Heroin – to obtain the same effect.
2. The minimum courtesy to expect when detailing your Symptoms to other Hypochondriacs. Never mention your really creative Symptoms, though – they may pinch them.

TOMORROW'S WORLD Essential viewing for all Hypochondriacs. Make it a point of honour to be in the Doctor's surgery the morning after every show, demanding the latest medical breakthrough featured in the programme.

-TOMY Suffix implying a surgical operation in which a cut or incision is used to open part of the body – e.g.:

Laparotomy – the opening-up of the abdominal cavity
Thoracotomy – the opening-up of the chest
Tracheotomy – the opening-up of the throat

Hypochondrotomy – the opening-up of a large can of worms.

TONGUE The busiest organ in a Hypochondriac's body.

TONSILLECTOMY Surgical Excision of the tonsils. This is now done less frequently due to SIDE EFFECTS – e.g., elderly relatives telling you at great length how they had theirs whipped out on the kitchen table.

'TOP DOCTOR' Supposedly one of the top men in the field. Don't be fooled into thinking this guy is good – Top Doctor is a tabloid term that means 'This was the only Doctor we could get to talk to us.'
  NB: As an example of blatant discrimination, Top Female Doctors are usually referred to only as 'Lady Doctors'.

TORTICOLLIS# A Doctor-impressing word for a Cricked Neck.

TOXIN A biological, poisonous protein made by virulent BACTERIA, venomous snakes and some mushrooms or toadstools. Botulinum Toxin is found in some improperly canned foods, so you could claim that's what you're suffering from next time you're improperly canned.

TOXOCARIASIS A human Infestation with dog worms, the larvae of which travel to the lungs, liver, brain or back of the eye to barricade themselves in. If you think you're suffering from this, ask your Doctor to prescribe Bob Martin's. (And if you get a kick out of that, ask him to prescribe Doc Marten's.)

TOXOPLASMOSIS A Disease caught from eating undercooked meat or handling infected cats – or indeed eating undercooked cats.

TRACTION The art of pulling you both ways to treat a fracture of the thigh bone or to immobilise a spinal Injury. May also be useful in treating SHORTNESS – unless it is of the breath, in which case it won't help at all.

TRAIT Any inherited characteristic or condition – e.g., eye colour, nose shape, degree of HYPOCHONDRIASIS. A Hypochondriac is partly born and partly made. You inherit your low threshold for Pain, your inborn errors of METABOLISM and your acute tendency to Panic Attacks. On top of these, you learn your love of an audience, your scepticism of orthodox medicine and the SIDE EFFECTS you can safely attribute to MEDICATION.

TRANQUILLISERS You either love 'em or hate 'em. The zombie-like state they induce receives plenty of sympathy, but the danger of Tranquillisers is that they may dampen down your Symptoms and ANXIETY to levels at which you can no longer enjoy them.

TRANSMISSIBLE The ability to be passed on whether as an Infection or as an inherited TRAIT. HYPOCHONDRIASIS is highly Contagious, Infectious and Transmissible. The spores are in the air and on the pages of every health magazine and newspaper. The fruiting bodies appear regularly on *News at Ten*, BBC2 documentaries, *Tomorrow's World* and Radio 4. Unfortunately, many CONSULTANTS make Hypochondriacs Transmissible by passing them on to another Consultant at increasingly short intervals.

TRANSPLANT The OPERATION all Hypochondriacs aspire to. If you have one, not only does it definitely mean that your Symptoms are being taken seriously – it also opens up the possibility of worrying about your donor's medical history as well as your own.

TRANSSEXUAL A person who feels uncomfortable with the sex they are born with, and prefers to live as a member of the opposite sex. For a Hypochondriac, becoming a Transsexual opens up a whole new field of gender-related Symptoms.

TRAUMA Any Physical Injury or Severe Emotional Shock – like being given a Clean Bill of Health.

TREMOR An involuntary, rhythmic shake of the hands, feet, jaw, tongue or head. If you notice you have a Tremor, first check that you are not sitting on the washing machine in its final spin. Then consider a differential Diagnosis of an overactive Thyroid, an inherited, familiar Tremor, Phaeochromocytoma, HANGOVER or withdrawal of Alcohol. If possible, claim to have an Essential Familial Tremor – this has the benefit of being temporarily relieved by small amounts of Alcohol. This could be just the excuse you've been looking for to set up an Intravenous Drip of gin.

TRICHOBEZOAR# A wonderful Doctor-impressing word to describe a hairball found in the stomach of anyone who nervously pulls, sucks or chews their hair. It forms in a similar manner to that mini-hamster you always find in the plug after you've washed your hair in the bath.

TRICHOTILLOMANIA The constant pulling out of one's own hair. Hypochondriacs may suffer from this themselves, but are more likely to induce it in their medical attendants.

TRIPLE THERAPY A magic combination of Antibiotics and Bismuth that kills all known Germs – and several unknown ones – dead. This form of guerrilla warfare is aimed against Helicobacter, the agent known to cause stomach Ulcers and even stomach Cancer. All Hypochondriacs should receive Triple Therapy at least once – though of course you shouldn't allow it to stop you from complaining about your Symptoms.

TUBERCULOSIS (TB) An infectious disease that is once again becoming increasingly common. This is a beautiful condition for Hypochondriacs because, although it usually affects the lung:

It can occur anywhere in the body
It can spread to every organ
It can cause a myriad of different Symptoms
It is difficult to diagnose
It can lie dormant for many years before reactivating.

If you notice Weight Loss, Night Sweats, Swollen Glands or a Low Grade FEVER, assume you have TB until proven otherwise – 30 million people are infected worldwide.

TUMOUR# Doctor-impressing word for a Lump.
TIP: If your Doctor makes a house call and you offer him a cup of tea, don't say, 'One Tumour or two?'

TYLECTOMY 1. An even better word for LUMPECTOMY. You can virtually be certain that your Doctor has never heard of this one.
2. Nicking lead off the church roof.

TYSS Stands for 'Told You So' Syndrome. Very useful for Hypochondriacs on those rare occasions when your Doctor actually finds you to be suffering from the Disease whose Symptoms you brought to the surgery.

U

ULCER An open sore on the skin or mucous MEMBRANES. These are generally due to injury, INFECTION, poor Blood Supply or CANCER. Most Hypochondriacs develop Aphthous Ulcers of the mouth at least once per year. If these are on the tip of the tongue, they're supposed to indicate you've been lying. Deny this strenuously, and insist it's at the very least a MALIGNANT LESION.

ULTRASOUND A clever TEST in which inaudible Sound Waves are passed through the body to bounce off tissue planes. Ultrasound has been used to detect Cholelithiasis, Cysts and PREGNANCY. If your doctor claims to have located the Loch Ness Monster inside you, then it's his idea of a joke. Laugh dutifully – it'll make the Ultrasound go all wobbly.

UREA A poisonous waste substance formed from the breakdown of Dietary Proteins. This is excreted via the KIDNEYS into the urine. A lucrative spin-off industry uses urea in moisturising creams and ointments to soften dry, scaly skin. Next time you're asked for a Urine Sample for TESTS, make sure it's not being sold to the private sector for the manufacture of cosmetics.

URETHRA The tube leading from the bladder to the outside world. In females, the urethra is only about 2cm long, so bugs travel up to cause Cystitis more easily. The male urethra is about 20cm long, though many men have the delusion that it's longer than this.

-URIA Suffix meaning 'in the urine' – e.g.:

Proteinuria – Protein in the urine
Haematuria – Blood in the urine
Glycosuria – Sugar in the urine
Lagerlouturia – Beer in the urine

URINARY RETENTION A build-up of urine in the bladder due to an outflow obstruction. This might mean a Bladder Stone, an enlarged PROSTATE GLAND, a TUMOUR or a PHIMOSIS. Alternatively, you might have a nerve problem, so the bladder forgets to contract. This is a great condition for a Hypochondriac – lots of lovely TESTS, and if you're lucky, a chance to experience the agonies of passing a catheter.

URINE SAMPLE Something any Hypochondriac will readily supply at the drop of a knicker. In fact, the truly committed Hypochondriac never goes anywhere without carrying a Urine Sample in a little pot in his or her pocket. Doctors often request a sample of Mid-Stream Urine – i.e., not just when you're starting or just when you're finishing. Collecting this is not as easy as it sounds – and you'll certainly need to wash your hands afterwards!

URTICARIA Allergic, itchy, raised LESIONS on the skin that are commonly known as Nettle Rash. If you get these, you are probably allergic to a DRUG, cosmetic, FOOD ADDITIVE or your sexual partner. You need HYDROCORTISONE which is great – you can then start worrying about SIDE EFFECTS of thinning the skin. When your sexual partner says he or she can see right through you, then you know you're winning.

UVULA The blobby thing that dangles at the back of the throat. Keep an eye on it – though it's unlikely to cause any problems, it's useful to watch to induce self-hypnosis. Also useful in a RORSCHACH TEST when you get bored with saying the ink blots remind you of Cancer cells.

V

VACCINE Bits and pieces of killed BACTERIA and VIRUSES injected to stimulate the IMMUNE SYSTEM. The ones to worry about are Live Vaccinations – these often reactivate inside a Hypochondriac to cause the very Disease you worried about catching in the first place. If this happens, you are fully justified in invoking the TYSS.

VAGINA The most mysterious and coveted passage on earth. You've heard of PENIS Envy – this is the bit that spawns the male equivalent. It is perhaps because men once descended from one of these that they spend so much of their adult life trying to get back up.

VAGINAL DISCHARGE An affliction of female Hypochondriacs that few male Doctors take seriously. As a noted – and typically callous – GYNAECOLOGIST once remarked, if a woman didn't have a Vaginal Discharge, she'd start to squeak when she walked.

VAGINISMUS Painful contraction and spasm of the vaginal muscles whenever a PENIS is in the vicinity. A common Symptom of FRIGIDITY – though not fancying the bloke is commoner.

VALSALVA'S MANOEUVRE A forcible attempt to breathe out when the airway is closed – e.g., when straining at a large constipated stool. This occasionally causes fainting, so the toilet is a more dangerous place than you thought. It also raises the question 'Who the hell was Valsalva?' and 'What on earth was he doing when he got this manoeuvre named after him?'

VARICOCOELE Scrotal Varicose Veins. One in fifteen men do not have the enormous TESTICLES they think they have. The extra padding is due to these.

VARICOSE VEINS Enlarged, dilated and twisted veins in which gravity acting on the weight of blood inside has caused a valve blow-out. These are a useful accoutrement for Hypochondriacs, as they inevitably ache, drag or swell during the day. If you're particularly careless and knock them, they also bleed torrentially. Although you're unlikely to get them operated on in today's NHS, it's worth putting your name on the waiting list so you can talk for some years about your impending OPERATION.

VAS DEFERENS The tubes cut during a VASECTOMY. A surgeon can try cobbling them back together (see REVERSAL OF VASECTOMY), but it probably won't make a Vas Deferens.

VASECTOMY The kindest cut of all, if you already have enough children. One of the most frustrating Complications of male Vasectomy is the partner's subsequent Pregnancy.

VD A Sexually TRANSMISSIBLE Disease. Hypochondriacs tend to avoid this, as contracting a Venereal Disease can imply an element of guilt, and you don't want to go to the surgery with any Symptoms that might concede the moral high ground to your Doctor. You're the one who should be looking righteous and reproachful when he can't make a Diagnosis.

VEGETARIAN DIET Not really faddy enough for the true Hypochondriac. Your Special Diet should be necessitated by some obscure ALLERGY rather than something as tenuous as mere principle. However, a Vegetarian Diet can produce a satisfying list of SIDE EFFECTS – e.g., BORBORYGMI, FLATUS, Halitosis.

VENEPUNCTURE The art of drawing blood with a needle and syringe. With a bit of luck you'll end up with a nasty BRUISE which can then be investigated for Thrombocytopaenia (Low Platelet Count).

VENESECTION The art of drawing loads of blood for donation or therapeutic purposes. The point at which VENEPUNCTURE becomes Venesection is not clear, but if you're giving more than half a pint feel free to demand a digestive biscuit, a cup of tea and a little badge.

VENTRICULAR FIBRILLATION This is a LIFE-THREATENING HEART ARRHYTHMIA that is followed by an ominous FLAT LINE on the MACHINE THAT GOES PING! Not a good one to pick unless you enjoy flirting with Death. Your chances of telling the tale are only fifty-fifty.

VERRUCA The Latin name for a WART. For some reason, this is only used to describe Warts on the sole of the foot. Jocularly described as a 'Bikini Bimbo', because it tends to get picked up round swimming pools.

VESICLE* A fluid-filled Blister which is a gift to a Hypochondriac, because it could mean:

The first recurrence of SMALLPOX
An attack of Chickenpox
Hand, Foot and Mouth Disease
Impetigo
Herpes
Shingles
Syphilis
LEPROSY
Rare Diseases of the IMMUNE SYSTEM

Tight-fitting shoes
Too much screw-driving.

Any one of these – except the last two – is worth having.

VIABILITY The capacity for independent survival and development. A human foetus is viable from around twenty-three weeks' Gestation with the help of Intensive Medical Care. A Hypochondriac should ensure their Symptoms are viable for at least two weeks. Two years is optimal.

VIBRATION WHITE FINGER An Occupational Hazard due to working with vibrating machinery – e.g., power drills, chainsaws. Doctors tend to be unsympathetic if you claim you got a White Finger from using your electric toothbrush – they're likely just to tell you to go and wash the toothpaste off.

VIRILISM The development in a woman of male characteristics, which can cause great anguish to the female sufferer. Not to be confused with FEMINISM, which can cause great anguish to the male sufferer.

VIRULENT Describes how rapidly and nastily a Microorganism can induce Disease. Virulent is the absolute minimum condition that a Hypochondriac should go for. If you can persuade it to become FULMINANT all the better.

VIRUS The smallest identified type of Infectious Agent. Viruses work by hijacking the machinery in our own cells and directing it to produce more Viruses rather than bits of human. The good news about them for Hypochondriacs is that they open up all kinds of possibilities for new Diseases. The bad news is that the average GP's average Diagnosis now tends to be a dismissive shrug, accompanied by the words, 'It's probably a Virus'. See TALOIA.

VISITING TIME The moment of glory, when the Hypochondriac who has achieved the accolade of ADMISSION TO HOSPITAL can hold court. Once your visitors have handed over their grapes, they're almost honour-bound to ask, 'How're you feeling?' – and then you have *carte blance* to *tell* them.

VISUAL ACUITY The sharpness of your eyes. As with Hearing, it's often useful to let Doctors think you can see/hear less than you can. That way, you often pick up snippets about your condition from:

Eavesdropping on conversations between the CONSULTANT and Medical Students on ward rounds
Hearing the Registrar bawl out the Houseman
Overhearing the Sister explain your DRUGS to the cleaner who dishes them out – staff shortages are CHRONIC these days
Reading your notes upside-down

Learn to decipher what your Doctor writes on the prescription pad – if pharmacists can do it, so can you.

VITAL SIGNS 1. Indicators that a person is still alive.
2. Essential basic Symptoms that all Hypochondriacs develop to fit the Diseases they aspire to.

VITAMINS Essential substances needed for the smooth functioning of the METABOLISM. If your Doctor offers you these, he is at least trying to take you seriously. Now is the time to bring in your OPPORTUNISTIC SYMPTOM.

VOMITING The reflex, involuntary emptying of the stomach. This is often preceded by Nausea, Sweating, Pallor, Excessive Drooling and a slowing of the Heart Rate. There are ways and ways of Vomiting. A Hypochondriac should avoid discreet deliveries in the bathroom and go for as wide a splatter as possible.

W

WAITING LIST It should be a point of honour for every Hypochondriac to be permanently on at least one Waiting List for some unspecified but ominously hinted-at OPERATION.

WAITING ROOM, DOCTOR'S The Hypochondriac's natural environment. It is here that you can:

A) Hold court about your own Symptoms
B) Listen out for other people's Symptoms which might come in handy for you some time.

WARD SISTER A strong-willed and beady-eyed woman, inordinately suspicious of all Symptoms that do not show, whose aim in life is to get patients out of the beds in her ward as soon as possible. Obviously, the Hypochondriac's natural enemy. See 'MAD COW' DISEASE.

WARDS, UNEXPECTED CLOSURE OF An increasingly prevalent hazard for the contemporary Hypochondriac. You've just got yourself all psyched up for Admission when the ADMINISTRATOR phones with some feeble story about running out of beds. Since half the wards are filled with second-rate Hypochondriacs, they should turf one of them out to accommodate a real professional like you.

WARTS Warts may not look very interesting, but remember – any one of them could develop into a MALIGNANT MELANOMA at any moment.

WATERHOUSE-FRIDERICHSEN SYNDROME A LIFE-THREATENING COMPLICATION of MENINGITIS, in which

Blood Clotting abnormalities cause bleeding into the adrenal glands. This causes profound SHOCK, which is good news as it means you'll get two full-time NURSES and half a Doctor all to yourself in INTENSIVE CARE. Though pretty unpleasant, Waterhouse-Friderichsen Syndrome is worth having for the name alone.

WATERWORKS Doctor's jocular expression which suggests he's not taking you seriously enough. If he asks, 'Any trouble with the old Waterworks?', reply coldly, 'I assume you're referring to Problems of the Urinary Tract.'

WHEEZE 1. A whistling noise made by tight airways when breathing out.
2. Prank perpetrated by MEDICAL STUDENTS, almost always involving a skeleton or CADAVER, and absolutely always involving a Rectal Glove.

WHITE COAT A garment worn to hide a Doctor's feelings of insecurity. Anyone wearing one of these has *carte blanche* to:

> Stick a finger up your bum before shaking your hand
> Ask personal details about your sex life
> Take off all your clothes
> Explore your anatomy with his own. See PALPATION.

Always ask to see some identification from a man in a White Coat before exposing your own credentials. He might just be a baker with a dirty mind.

WHITE COAT HYPERTENSION The sudden surging rise in Blood Pressure at the sight of a Doctor wearing a White Coat. Common in many human types, but not Hypochondriacs, who usually feel so relieved at finally seeing a Doctor that their Blood Pressure actually falls.

WIND-UP Doctor referring you to an undertaker for measurement after you've come into his surgery complaining of a hangnail.

WORD BLINDNESS The inexplicable fumbling for a Symptom that occasionally hits even the most experienced Hypochondriac put on the spot by an unexpected confrontation with a Doctor in Marks & Spencer.

WORK-RELATED UPPER LIMB DISORDER# Doctor-impressing expression for REPETITIVE STRAIN INJURY.

WORST-CASE SCENARIO The Hypochondriac's basic assumption.

X

X CHROMOSOME Something every female Hypochondriac has two of whilst males must cope with one. This chromosome carries femaleness – and is responsible for the fact that males are saddled with nipples.

XXY SYNDROME Also known as Klinefelter's Syndrome, this is on the whole one to avoid unless you're playing Scrabble. As the most common Sex Chromosome Abnormality, it is inadvisable to claim this, unless you want to admit to small, non-functioning TESTICLES, hairy ears and a tendency to take holidays at Her Majesty's pleasure.

XXX SYNDROME Also known as Superfemale Syndrome. Unfortunately, this one is not as good a bet as it sounds. Victims have underdeveloped sexual organs, don't menstruate and are usually mentally challenged (i.e., 'retarded' for those of you who don't understand about Political Correctness).

XXXY SYNDROME Like the XXY SYNDROME, only worse. The PENIS is minuscule, and the IQ matches it.

XXXX SYNDROME A problem most Australians wouldn't give a lager for.

XANTHELASMA Yellow, fatty deposits round the eyes that are linked with abnormally high blood fats. If you have Xanthelasma, start worrying about your increased risk of MYOCARDIAL INFARCTION. If you don't have any and would like some, the make-up department of your local playhouse should be able to help.

XEROPHTHALMIA Dry Eye resulting from a lack of Vitamin A. The word is used by skilled Hypochondriacs to describe the effect of the full recounting of their Symptoms – 'Not a Xerophthalmia in the house'.

X-RAYS Invisible Electromagnetic Energy Waves that pass through the body and produce images of internal tissues on a Radiographic Plate. Highly complex – but a Hypochondriac needs regular exposure to X-rays in order to:

Maintain your requisite quota of TESTS
Maintain your credibility
Ensure your Symptoms are still spot-on and medically convincing
Keep your risk of X-ray-induced CANCER at a respectably high level.

X-RAY PLATES What the conscientious Hypochondriac has framed over his or her mantelpiece.

Y

YAWS A tropical Disease similar to Syphilis, which is not sexually transmitted. Soon after Infection, a large, itchy, raspberry-like GROWTH occurs. Scratching spreads the Infection and triggers more Growths on the skin. Not a suitable subject for discussion in a pub, as the simple inquiry 'What's Yaws?' can lead to a disproportionately large bar bill.

Y CHROMOSOME The sex chromosome that supplies the information to make a male – so named because so many women over the years have asked 'Y?'

YELLOW NAILS SYNDROME A Disease in which nails are thickened, slow-growing and yellow. It is linked with Bronchitis or Oedema of the legs, and is due to Blockage of the Lymph System. Before complaining to your Doctor of this, do check that you're not a cigarette smoker.

YELLOW FEVER A severe Viral Infection transmitted by a love-biting mosquito. JAUNDICE develops after FEVER, HEADACHES and EPISTAXIS. KIDNEY Failure, Delirium, COMA and DEATH often follow. Vaccination protects you for ten years, but a true Hypochondriac will always worry that the Vaccine didn't take, or – this is a good one – that the Virus has Mutated.

YOGA A relaxation technique in which the aim is to tie yourself in knots by putting your ankles behind your ears. This is a brilliant way to dislocate joints, sprain ligaments and strain muscles.

Z

ZINC A Mineral essential for normal Growth, Sexual Development, Wound Healing and for a healthy PROSTATE GLAND. Zinc controls the activity of over one hundred Enzymes, and most of us can't get enough of it. The commonest symptom of Zinc Deficiency is LACK OF TASTE, so we all know plenty of people suffering from that.

ZOONOSIS Any Disease caught from an animal. The long list includes Leptospirosis, Cat Scratch Fever, Toxocariasis, TOXOPLASMOSIS, RABIES, RINGWORM, Tapeworms, Psittacosis and possibly BSE. It does not, however include Hives, Moles, Crabs, Mussel Weakness or Feeling Husky.

ZYGOTE You, when you were approximately thirty minutes old, measured 0.1mm across and consisted of a single, fertilised ovum. Who'd have thought then that you'd grow up to be the ultimately accomplished Hypochondriac you are now!

APPENDIX I

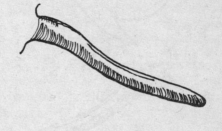

GRUMBLING APPENDIX